Days at the
Morisaki Bookshop

ABOUT THE AUTHOR

Satoshi Yagisawa was born in Chiba, Japan, in 1977. Days at the Morisaki Bookshop, his debut novel, was originally published in 2009 and won the Chiyoda Literature Prize.

Days at the Morisaki Bookshop

SATOSHI
YAGISAWA

Translated from the Japanese
by Eric Ozawa

MANILLA
PRESS

First published in the UK in 2023 by
MANILLA PRESS
An imprint of Bonnier Books UK
4th Floor, Victoria House, Bloomsbury Square, London, WC1B 4DA
Owned by Bonnier Books
Sveavägen 56, Stockholm, Sweden

Originally published as 森崎書店の日々 in Japan in 2010 by
Shogakukan Inc.

A CIP catalogue record for this book is
available from the British Library.

ISBN: 978–1–78658–323–9

Also available as an ebook and an audiobook

5 7 9 10 8 6 4

Typeset by Envy Design Ltd
Printed and bound in Great Britain by Clays Ltd, Elcograf S.p.A.

Designed by Leah Carlson-Stanisic
Artwork by Ksusha Dusmikeeva and GoodStudio at Shutterstock, Inc.

Manilla Press is an imprint of Bonnier Books UK
www.bonnierbooks.co.uk

Part One

1

From late summer to early spring the next year, I lived at the Morisaki Bookshop. I spent that period of my life in the spare room on the second floor of the store, trying to bury myself in books. The cramped room barely got any light, and everything felt damp. It smelled constantly of musty old books.

But I will always remember the days I spent there. Because that's where my real life began. And I know, without a doubt, that if not for those days, the rest of my life would have been bland, monotonous, and lonely.

The Morisaki Bookshop is precious to me. It's a place I know I'll never forget.

When I close my eyes, the memories still come back to me so vividly.

It all began like a bolt of lightning out of the clear blue sky. No, what happened was more shocking than that, more shocking even than seeing frogs raining from the sky in a downpour.

One day, Hideaki, the boyfriend I'd been going out with for a year, suddenly blurted out, "I'm getting married."

When I first heard him, my mind was filled with questions. Now, if he'd said, "Let's get married," I would've understood. Or if he'd said, "I want to get married," I still would've understood. But "I'm getting married" was just weird. Marriage, after all, is a covenant based on mutual agreement, so grammatically the sentence was completely wrong. And what about the casual way he said it? It was so brusque. The tone of his voice was exactly the same one he would've used to say, "Hey, I found one hundred yen on the side of the road."

It was a Friday night in the middle of June. We were having a nice dinner together after work at an Italian restaurant in Shinjuku. The restaurant was on the top floor of a hotel, so we had a beautiful view of the city at night, all the gleaming neon lights. It was our favorite spot.

Hideaki, who was three years ahead of me at work, was someone I'd had a secret crush on from the day I started. Just being together made my heart bounce inside my chest like a trampoline. That night was the first time we'd been alone together in a while, so as I drank my wine, I was in an especially good mood.

But then . . .

Without thinking, I replied, "Huh?" I thought maybe I had misheard him. But he repeated what he'd said, matter-of-factly. "So, it looks like I'm getting married next year."

"Married? Who's getting married to whom?"

"I am. To her."

"Huh?" I was still puzzled. "Who's she?"

And then, he says the name of a girl in a different department of the company—without the slightest hint of guilt in his voice. She had been hired at the same time as me, and she looked so pretty that even I wanted to wrap my arms around her.

Compared to her, I was taller and more ordinary-looking. I couldn't understand why he'd even consider getting involved with me when he was going out with someone as pretty as she was.

When I asked him, he said they'd been together for two and a half years. In other words, they'd been together even longer than we had. Of course, I had no idea that he was with anyone else. I never suspected it. I never considered the possibility. We'd kept our relationship a secret at the office, but I had just assumed that was to avoid making things awkward for others at work. Yet, from the very beginning, I was never his first choice, I was just someone to fool around with. How did I not realize that? Either I was slow—or there was something off about him.

Anyway, the two of them had already met each other's parents. The engagement gifts would be done next month. I felt dizzy. It was as if a monk had rung a temple bell inside my head. I could almost hear the gong.

"So, having the wedding in June would be great, right, but she didn't ask, and now, of course, it's too late for this year, which is why . . ."

I sat there in a daze listening to the words coming out of his mouth. Then, I muttered, "Oh, that's good." Even I was surprised by what I'd said.

"Oh, thanks, but you know we can still see each other sometimes," he said with a big smile. It was his usual smile—how sporting of him. He didn't have a care in the world.

In a melodrama this would've been my moment to get up and throw my wine in his face. But I'd never been good at expressing my feelings like that. It's only once I'm alone, mulling things over, that I can figure out what on earth I'm really feeling. And besides, the temple bell ringing inside my head was getting too loud to think.

Still in a daze, I said goodbye to him and went back to my apartment alone. And when I finally regained my presence of mind, I felt a sudden wave of grief come over me. Far more than anger, I felt grief. A grief that was so violent, so intensely palpable, that I felt like I could reach out and touch it.

Tears poured from my eyes. It felt like they would never stop. But no matter how much I cried, I couldn't seem to get a hold of myself. I hadn't even turned on the lights. I just collapsed in the middle of the room, sobbing. The dumb thought popped into my head that if only all these tears were oil, I'd be rich, but it was so dumb that it made me cry more.

Someone help me, I thought to myself. I was serious. But I couldn't raise my voice. I couldn't do anything but cry.

After that, it was just one awful thing after another.

Because we worked in the same office, I had to keep seeing him no matter how much I hated it. And he kept contacting me as much as ever, which was excruciating. And to make things worse, I was always running into his fiancée in the breakroom and the cafeteria. Whenever it happened, she would greet me with this radiant smile, and I couldn't tell whether or not she knew about us.

Before long, my stomach refused to take in any food. I couldn't sleep at night. My weight dropped precipitously. And, despite my attempts to hide it with makeup, my complexion became so pale that I looked like a corpse.

In the middle of work, tears would come streaming down my face. I cried so many times, hiding inside a stall in the bathroom, muffling the sound of my sobbing.

After two weeks of this, I'd reached my limit, physically and psychologically. I finally went to my supervisor and handed in my resignation.

On my last day of work, Hideaki came over and said in a cheery voice, "Just 'cause you quit, doesn't mean we can't get dinner, right?"

I had lost my boyfriend and my job all at once. I felt almost like I'd been cast off suddenly into outer space.

I'm from Kyushu and came to Tokyo for work after graduating

from a local college in the south. Because of that, the only people I knew in the city were basically the people from the office. And because I'm shy and have never been good at making friends, in all of Tokyo, there was no one I was close to.

When I look back, the word that sums up the life I'd lived up till this point, all twenty-five years of it, is "adequate." I was born to an adequately wealthy family, graduated from an adequately good school, got a job at an adequately good company.

Meeting Hideaki meant so much to me at the time. For someone as passive as I was then, finding a boyfriend like him was nothing short of a miracle. I liked him so much that I could barely stand it. The downside was I never saw this shock coming, and I had no idea how to cope with it.

The coping mechanism I ultimately went with was to devote my life to sleep. Even I was surprised by how sleepy I was. I know it was probably my body's way of helping me avoid reality, but once I buried myself in my covers, I would fall asleep right away. I spent days in a deep sleep in my little room, drifting all alone through outer space.

I probably spent a month like that. I was ignoring my phone and then one night when I woke up, I noticed I had a voicemail. I didn't recognize the number on the screen, but I gave it a listen. All of a sudden, I heard a cheerful voice saying, "Hey, hey!"

"Takako? How're you doing? It's me. It's Satoru! I'm calling from the bookshop. Give me a call. Later's fine. Oh damn, I got a customer. Gotta go. Talk soon."

I sat there for a moment, puzzled. *Satoru? Who?* I had absolutely no idea. He said my name, so it couldn't be a wrong number. What was the bookshop? Bookshop . . . I turned the word over again and again in my mind—and then it finally hit me.

Satoru was my uncle Satoru! Come to think of it, I had heard from my mother a while back that he'd taken over the bookshop in Jimbocho that my great-grandfather started. The last time I'd seen him I was in my first year of high school, so we hadn't seen each other in almost a decade, but I was sure that was his voice.

And then I had the sneaking suspicion that my mother was behind this. Yes, it had to be her. She was the only person I'd told that I'd quit my job and broken up with my boyfriend. She must have asked him for a favor because she was so worried about me. But even so, that wasn't a good enough reason.

To be honest, I wasn't really that fond of Uncle Satoru. He was so unconventional that he was hard to figure out. He was completely uninhibited, no matter who was around. He was always making little jokes and chuckling to himself. It was odd, and it made him come off as a bit of a weirdo, which bothered me.

But when I was little, I loved his personality. We used to play together in his room when my mother took me back with her to Tokyo to visit her family. But as I approached puberty, his eccentricity became extremely off-putting, and I started secretly avoiding him. And then, on top of that, he suddenly got married—even though he didn't have a steady job yet. From then on, one way or another, he seemed to cause trouble in the family.

That's why when I came to Tokyo I never once thought of going to see him. I was trying not to have anything to do with him.

The afternoon after I got his voicemail, I reluctantly called him back. I could just imagine my mother flying into a blind rage if I didn't return his call. Given that my uncle was in his midtwenties when I was in grade school, he must be already past forty.

On the very first ring, someone answered.

"Hello, this is the Morisaki Bookshop."

"Hi, it's me, Takako.

"Oh, hey!" I could hear my uncle shouting on the other end

of the line. That's the intensity I remember from the old days. I rushed to hold the phone away from my ear.

"It's been so long! You been okay?"

"Ah, yeah, well . . ."

"I knew you were in Tokyo, but you never came to visit me."

"Sorry about that. I've been busy with work," I apologized automatically.

"But you quit, didn't you?"

He cut to the quick. I mumbled a response. This was not a man you could expect delicacy from. My uncle just kept on talking, telling me how this was just like the old days, talking on and on—until he suddenly came out and said, "Listen, I've been thinking, if you don't feel like working right now, how about you come and stay here?"

"Sorry?" His sudden offer caught me off guard.

But my uncle kept pressing me for an answer. "The money you're spending on rent and utilities is nothing to sneeze at. If you come here, it's all free. Well, I mean you could maybe help me out a little at the bookshop."

When I asked him about it, he explained that he was running the shop all by himself. He needed someone to open up in the mornings for him while he went to his appointments at the hospital to be treated for his back pain. My uncle lived in a house in Kunitachi, so I'd have the place to myself when the shop was closed. He assured me I'd have total privacy. The place had been a residence until some years ago, so it was fully equipped with a proper bathroom.

I thought it over for a moment. I knew my current arrangement couldn't last forever. If I kept on living this way, I was going to run out of money soon. On the other hand, I didn't like the idea of anyone interfering in my life.

"But I'm sure I'd be imposing," I said, attempting to decline the offer.

My uncle did not take the hint at all.

"Imposing? That's nonsense. It would be my pleasure to have you."

Did Aunt Momoko agree too? I started to ask the question, but I quickly caught myself. That's right. His wife, Momoko, had gone and left him years ago. It was a pretty big deal in our family. When she ran off, he seemed so depressed that my mother was really worried his health might suffer too. I remember feeling sorry for my uncle when I heard the news, but it left me with a strange feeling. It didn't make sense. At their wedding, the two of them had seemed so deeply in love. Aunt Momoko was so kind and good-natured. She was hardly the kind of person who seemed likely to run off.

I was remembering all this and mumbling my way through the conversation. My uncle, meanwhile, was trying to rush ahead with the plan. "Great. It's decided then."

I tried again to hold him off. "But what about all my things?" I said, but he told me he had space in his house in Kunitachi for all that. I could send everything there and just take some smaller bags with me to the shop.

It looked like I'd been outmaneuvered on all fronts.

"Trust me, Takako. This'll be better for you too."

But how was I supposed to trust someone I hadn't seen in a decade?

"Well, I'll start getting things ready over here," my uncle said, and then, without waiting for a response, he told me a customer had just come in and we'd have to talk later. Then he hung up.

I sat there for a while in a daze, listening to the dial tone.

2

Two weeks later, I was standing in Jimbocho Station. How had it come to this? In an instant, my life had changed so quickly that I was still reeling from it.

After the conversation with my uncle, I had a phone call with my mother. "What'll it be?" she asked. "Come back to Kyushu or go to Satoru's place?" I reluctantly chose my uncle's. I knew that if I went back home, I'd probably be pushed into an arranged marriage, and I'd never come back here again. After all the trouble I'd gone through to move to Tokyo, I couldn't stand the idea of going back like that and admitting that it had all been a total failure.

Being outside for the first time in a long while, I felt unsteady on my feet. But I made it to Jimbocho on the train somehow. Yet the moment I came aboveground from the subway, I felt fierce sunlight bearing down on me. The rainy season had completely given way to summer while I was asleep. Above my head, the sun was glaring down at me like a teenage boy. When I'd quit my job, the real heat of summer still seemed far away. It made me a little sad—even the seasons were betraying me.

This was the first time I'd ever been to Jimbocho. My grandfather's house was in Kunitachi, an hour to the west, so we didn't have much reason to come here.

For a moment, I stood at the traffic signal at an intersection, turning around and around, trying to take everything in.

It all looked so strange.

I saw a main avenue (which my uncle had told me was Yasukuni

Street), and all along it on both sides were rows of bookshops. Everywhere you turned, there was another bookshop.

Now, normally one would be enough for a street. Here, however, the majority of the stores were bookshops. While your eye might have been drawn at first to the bigger ones like Sanseidō and Shosen, what really stood out were the small used bookshops. Seeing them all in a row together had its own subtle impact. On the other side of the street, towards Suidōbashi, there were a few large office buildings, but they only ended up making the place seem even more bizarre.

Still confused, I crossed an intersection that was crowded with salarymen on their lunch break and walked down the street of bookshops. Following my uncle's directions, I left the main road and turned into a little backstreet called Sakura. This brought me to an area of secondhand bookshops.

I murmured to myself, "This is a wonderland of secondhand books."

As I stood there getting broiled in the hot sun, trying to figure out how I was going to find my uncle's store, I noticed a man looking my way, waving his hands in the air. His hair was messy; he was wearing black, thick-framed glasses, and he was so skinny and small that he seemed boyish. He'd thrown on a short-sleeved checked shirt, loose cotton pants, and some sandals. I definitely recognized that look. It was my uncle Satoru.

His whole face lit up as he said, "Hey, Takako, that is you after all."

Up close, I could see my uncle had aged a lot. There was no hiding the deep wrinkles around his eyes. His skin, once as white as some ill-fated damsel in a fairytale, was now marked by a phenomenal number of sunspots. But behind his glasses, you could see that strange, childlike glint in his eye.

"Were you waiting for me out in front of the store all this time?"

"I thought this was around when you'd show up. You know the whole area is just one secondhand bookshop after another, and I figured I can't have you getting lost, right? So I came out to wait for you. All this time I was expecting a schoolgirl in uniform, but at some point, I guess, you must've grown up."

It made sense. The last time I'd seen him I was in my first year of high school. We'd come up to Tokyo for the first anniversary of my grandfather's passing. It had been almost ten years since then. He was still the same though. He might be over forty now, but he still had that same breezy way about him. He was the exact opposite of anyone's idea of a dignified man. Which was something I absolutely couldn't stand about him when I was teenager. I was so sensitive then about gauging the distance between other people and me.

After I stopped staring at my uncle, I turned to look at the storefront.

"So this is the shop my great-grandfather started."

I stared at the shop with its sign that read MORISAKI BOOK-SHOP: SPECIALIZING IN LITERATURE OF THE MODERN ERA and felt a little moved by the sight. Even though I'd never met my great-grandfather, I still thought it was a pretty big deal that my uncle was the third generation in our family to carry on the tradition.

The shop was about thirty years old, but it looked like something from an earlier era. Through the glass doors of the little two-floor wooden building, you could see the books crammed together.

"The original shop was on Suzuran Street back in the Taishō era. Of course, it's gone now, so I guess this is sort of the second Morisaki Bookshop."

"Wow."

"Well, come in, come in."

My uncle practically yanked my luggage out of my hands and ushered me into the shop. The instant I stepped inside I was hit by a musty smell.

I accidentally said the word "musty" out loud.

My uncle laughed and corrected me. "Do me a favor and try to imagine it as the dampness after a morning rain."

Everywhere you looked there were books. In this small room that barely saw the sun, everything seemed suffused with the scent of the Shōwa era. Paperbacks and hardcovers were packed tightly on the well-organized bookshelves. The larger collections of complete works were piled up in stacks along the wall. Even the area behind the little counter with the register was full of books. If there were ever a big earthquake, it would undoubtedly all fall down, and you'd be buried beneath an avalanche of books.

"How many books do you have here?" I asked, half in shock.

"I'd say roughly about six thousand."

"Six thousand!" I shrieked.

"This place is small, so that's pretty much the limit."

"What does that mean, 'specializing in literature of the modern era'?"

"We concentrate on modern Japanese authors. Come here. Look."

At my uncle's urging, I scanned the spines of the books lined up on the shelves. There were authors whose names I recognized like Ryūnosuke Akutagawa, Sōseki Natsume, Ōgai Mori, but mostly it was authors I'd never heard of before. And the ones I'd heard of, I only knew from what I'd read in class in high school.

"So, um, you collect books from all these authors?" I said.

My uncle laughed. "Most of the bookshops around here deal

primarily in one specific field or type of book. There are stores for scholarly books. There are stores that only handle scripts for plays. There are also some more unusual shops that only deal in stuff like old postcards and photographs. This neighborhood has the largest concentration of secondhand bookshops in the world."

"In the world?"

"Yeah. Because back in the Meiji era at the end of the nineteenth century and the beginning of the twentieth, the neighborhood was a center of culture, and it was loved by cultured people and writers. The reason there are so many bookstores is that they built a lot of schools in the neighborhood in that era, which meant there were suddenly all these stores selling scholarly books."

"It goes that far back?"

"Oh yeah, and that history continues uninterrupted to the present here. Writers like Ōgai Mori and Jun'ichirō Tanizaki wrote novels set here. Now, lots of tourists from overseas come."

He was talking about it with so much pride it was like it all belonged to him.

"I've been living in Tokyo, but I didn't have the slightest idea about this place," I said, frankly impressed. Honestly, that response from my uncle to my little question impressed me too. For someone everyone in my family thought was just drifting aimlessly, someone who never looked for a real job, he seemed to know a lot. It reminded me that back when I would go see him when I was young, his room was always filled with difficult books of history and philosophy.

"Next time, you should wander around a bit, check out the area. There are lots of interesting places. Let's leave it till another day though. Let me show you to your room first. The second floor is buried in books from the rest of the collection, but the room is big."

When we peeked into the room on the second floor, I almost fainted on the spot. This "collection" he'd mentioned turned out to be towering stacks of books all over the room. There wasn't anywhere to step inside. It was a scene straight out of a sci-fi movie set in a city of the not-so-distant future. An ancient air conditioner was running full blast, but one by one drops of sweat appeared on my skin. I could hear the piercing call of a cicada somewhere in the distance.

I turned to my uncle standing next to me and gave him an icy glare. What was he talking about when he said he was getting ready for me? There wasn't enough space for a mouse to stretch its legs in that room.

"Damn, I'd meant to organize things in there before you got here, but . . ." he said, rubbing the back of his head apologetically. "You see, I threw my back out three days ago. It's the bookseller's destiny, I'm afraid. But I did move half of the books over to the empty room next door. So if you just toss the remaining ones in there too, you should be right at home."

At that moment, we heard the sound of the glass door downstairs opening, and my uncle said, "Sorry about that," and ran back downstairs.

I looked around the room and sighed. "Toss" them in there, he said. Easy for him to say. I felt like I'd been duped. But I'd already broken the lease for my apartment, and I didn't have anywhere else to live. I prepared myself for the worst and started cleaning up the room.

For the entire day, I waged a war against those books. I was heaving huge piles into the room next door, dripping with sweat. But if I got even the slightest bit careless, my Towers of Babel would collapse, struck down by an angry God. Little by little, my intense hatred for those books grew stronger. Nevertheless, by evening, I'd somehow succeed in clearing out the majority of books into the empty room. I rescued the little table that had been buried in the avalanche. In the room next door, the books were piled to the ceiling. I was a little worried that the floor might collapse. But it seemed like a sturdy enough building, so I told myself it would be okay. Then I took out the vacuum and sucked up all the dust and bits of trash that had been floating above the ground like evil spirits. Once I had wiped down the walls and tatami mats with a dust cloth, the room started to look like someplace a human being might actually inhabit.

I was standing in the entrance to the room with my hands on my hips, surveying my work with some measure of satisfaction, when my uncle closed up the shop and came upstairs to see me.

"Whoa, you really cleaned things up. Amazing," he said. "Takako, I swear if you'd been born in England in the latter half of the nineteenth century, you could have been a brilliant maid." He went on saying more ridiculous things like that to me.

Oh God, I thought, *I'm going to have to get along with this person.*

"I'm tired and I'm going to bed," I said.

"Definitely, take it easy, get all the rest you need. Tomorrow morning you can help me out though, right?"

Once my uncle had left the shop, I got right into the bath, and then crawled into my musty-smelling futon without even drying my hair.

When I turned off the lights, the room suddenly fell completely silent. It was like all those books were absorbing the sound.

I looked up at the dim ceiling in a daze and started feeling hopeless. *Can I really stay here for a while? I don't see myself getting used to this.* But it only lasted a moment. One second later, I was snoring.

In my dream, I was an android maid living in a city in the not-so-distant future. In that neighborhood, all the buildings were made of used books.

When I opened my eyes the next morning, I had no idea where I was. I looked over at the alarm clock beside me. The time read 10:22.

All of a sudden, I came back to reality. "Ah!" I yelled and jumped out of bed. The store opens at ten. Before I went to bed I set my alarm for eight, but at some point it must have been turned off. *Who on earth played this cruel trick on me?* The culprit, of course, was me.

What a mess! I'd always been good at waking up on time. I'd been proud of the fact that in my three years at the company I was never once late. But here I was in my pajamas, with total bed head, hurrying down the stairs, rushing to push up the heavy metal shutter out front. As I did, the summer light poured into the room. All the stores facing the street were already open. I was clearly getting a late start.

What could I do? For about a half hour, I just sat stupidly at the counter in my pajamas, half-panicked. But to my surprise, no one came in.

Later on, it didn't seem that anyone was going to show up. There were some people walking down the street, but they walked right by. Feeling like an idiot, I casually went upstairs and changed my clothes, brushed my hair, and even put on a little makeup, and then came down again.

At around noon, people started to trickle in. But for the most part, they only bought the cheap fifty-yen or one-hundred-yen paperbacks. I found myself worrying whether the shop was going to make it. After stifling about thirty yawns, I dozed off a couple of times.

Around one, a middle-aged man turned up. He was short and stout and spectacularly bald. As soon as he saw me sitting behind the counter, he did a double take. "What? Where's Satoru—more importantly, who are you? Did they hire a girl to work part-time? But this place can't afford to hire anyone, can it?"

He hit me with one question after another. How could I describe him? He was the kind of middle-aged man who didn't hold anything back.

"Um, my uncle will be coming in around two. I'm his niece, Takako. I'm sort of part-time, I suppose. I'm working for room and board. As for the shop's financial situation, I'm afraid I'm not familiar with the details."

As I ran through my replies, the man studied me carefully with a look of deep interest.

"Oh wow," he said. "How did I not know that all this time Satoru had a cute, young niece."

I flashed a sweet smile. It was lucky for me he hadn't seen my shameful appearance this morning. Maybe he was a sweet old guy after all. He seemed pleasant enough, and what's more, he had good taste.

"So I was thinking about reading Naoya Shiga again. It's been a while. You know how my wife threw out most of mine a while ago."

He wandered around the bookshelves as he talked. How should I know what happened with his wife? I just met him today.

"Where are they again?"

"Where are what?"

"The Naoya Shiga books."

"Ah, well, um, they're probably somewhere around there."

The man suddenly gave me a stern look, as if he were trying to evaluate me.

"Are you a reader?"

"Definitely not."

In the instant I answered, my middle-aged companion transformed into a demon. His eyes lit up as he glared at me.

That is when his diatribe began. *Good grief.* "Young people today, they don't read books anymore. They just play computer games. It's hopeless. And even if they do read books, it's just manga or these shallow little stories on their cell phones. Even my son, he's almost thirty and he still just plays video games all the time. Is that okay? You think so? Absolutely not. They're only seeing the surface of things. And if you don't want to be a shallow person, then you should try reading some of the wonderful books in this place."

The man went on and on talking like this. When he finally went home, it was almost an hour later. In the end, his monologue went on so long that he left without buying anything. I was getting exhausted too. When my uncle showed up a half hour later, for a moment, he seemed like my savior.

"How was your first day? Any trouble?" he said. As he asked the question, he went straight to check the account ledger for the day.

"No," I said wearily. "But a little after noon, a guy came in. It was as if his head was a dandelion and all the fuzz blew away except for the sides. He talked a lot."

"Ah, that's Sabu. He's been a regular here for about twenty years."

I laughed in spite of myself. The name Sabu fit him perfectly.

"That guy, what can I say, he loves the great writers of Japanese literature from the bottom of his heart. But he's a talker. I get trapped sometimes too. But if you make a little tea, and nod and say 'oh' and 'ah' a little bit, he goes home."

Ah, I thought, there's a lot to the service industry. Even the notion of a regular customer seemed like a rare thing these days.

"By the way, Uncle . . ." I said, remembering my biggest question of the day.

"What is it?"

"Is the shop okay? There aren't that many customers. And the people who buy books only buy the cheap ones . . ."

My uncle laughed, sounding apparently happy.

"That's true. These days secondhand books don't sell well. Back when my father was young, the secondhand bookshops did incredible business. But the situation is different now. I mean the publishing industry wasn't like it is now, and there was no television. However, we started selling online six years ago. And sometimes we sell a sought-after book that goes for a lot of money. We're making it work somehow. And we have a good number of regular customers like Sabu, who have been with us since my father's time. Takako, don't you go to secondhand bookshops?"

"I go to BookOff sometimes. I can read manga there."

"These days it's just big chains like that. But in those places you're never going to find a book written by a writer from decades ago. There's no demand for it. Still, there are a lot of people in this world who love old books. There are even some girls your age. For people like that, this place is heaven. And I happen to be one of those people."

"I remember your room used to be filled with books. How long ago did you take over the store?"

"It was right after my father died. So almost ten years? But compared to the other shop owners around here, I'm just a spring chicken. They've all been running their bookshops for thirty, forty years."

"Wow. That's amazing. It's almost beyond comprehension."

"Takako, you should try to read some. You can read any of the books here," he said, smiling.

I just laughed.

3

I didn't oversleep again after that day, and somehow figured out
what to do in the store. Fortunately, business was mostly slow
until the afternoon. I would sit at the counter in the back and
zone out. My routine didn't change much once I'd settled in. I
would open up first thing in the morning, tend the store until
my uncle arrived and relieved me of duty. Then I would trudge
upstairs, bury myself in the covers of my futon, and sleep.

My room contained only the absolute bare necessities. I'm
sure it wouldn't have looked like much of a life to anyone else,
but it suited me. Honestly, in my frame of mind, I was ready to
leave behind the things of this world.

My uncle Satoru would appear after noon, dressed in the
slouchy, loose clothes that would never have been allowed at a
normal company. When he came in, he would first check the account ledger, and then the online orders, before getting on the
phone to chat about something or other for work.

I could hear him complaining to the person on the other end
of the phone, saying, "Nah, no way" or "That's pretty harsh, isn't
it?" or "If we don't make it through this . . ." He might have been
complaining about the situation the business was in, and yet
something about the tone of his voice always seemed happy.

What I didn't expect about the used-book business was how
big the network was. According to my uncle, the network of
booksellers and your personal relationships were a big part of
making sure you could bring in new inventory and keep the store

from running out of books. A specialty store like the Morisaki Bookshop couldn't maintain its inventory just by buying books that customers came in to sell. The periodic auctions that the bookstore union organized were crucial for stores to get more used books.

"Even though we think of it as an independent business, what matters in the industry more than anything are the relationships you have with people. I guess that's probably true of the world in general," he said, looking rather pleased with himself.

There was still a considerable gap, however, between the man proclaiming this to me and the image I had in my mind of a secondhand bookshop owner that came from my grandfather. My grandfather was hard-headed and inflexible, a man of few words. At family get-togethers, he sat imposingly at the center of the group, surrounded by all of our relatives. As a child I was secretly afraid of him, and my grandmother would always laugh and say, "He's an old used bookseller. That's just the way he is."

But compared to him, my uncle was as flexible and indecisive as a jellyfish. I'd never spent so much time with him before, but the more I did, the more I was surprised by how wishy-washy he was. I even got the wild idea that my aunt Momoko had run off because she'd gotten sick of it. And yet in spite of all that, the regular customers kept coming, ready to chitchat.

The two of us didn't talk much aside from work, but after about a week had passed, my uncle couldn't take it any longer. "Takako," he said with an amazed look on his face, "all you do is sleep. You're a sleep monster."

"I must be going through a sleepy phase," I replied coldly. My uncle was just itching to interfere in my life, but I refused to let him draw me out.

"At twenty-five?"

"That's right. It's like they say, 'a sleeping child is a growing child.'"

"But you have so much time. Why don't you try going for a walk? There are lots of interesting places. Listen, I've been coming here since I was a kid and I've never gotten tired of it."

"I'm okay. I'd rather sleep."

I could tell my uncle wasn't finished talking, but I put an end to the conversation. After that, no matter what he said, I wasn't going to reply. I was as silent as a stone. Deep down, I was sulking.

Of course, my uncle must have heard everything from my mother, so he more or less knew what was going on in my life. And yet despite that, he was just casually bringing up the subject without any consideration. It made me angry.

Even our regular customer Sabu seemed to know all about my life. He came in one day and said, "Oh, if it isn't the sleep monster, Takako."

"Who told you that?" I said, indignantly. But of course, it could only have been my uncle, the person I was really angry with.

"That you regularly sleep fifteen hours and you're still sleepy?"

"I don't sleep fifteen hours. More like thirteen."

When I corrected him, Sabu shook his head in amazement.

"When I was in my twenties, I couldn't spare that much time for sleep. I was always reading."

"When I decide to sleep, I sleep."

"You're stubborn, just like your uncle."

"That's absurd. How could you compare me to that fool?"

"You also have his peculiar sense of humor," Sabu said and giggled.

"I'm not like him. Please don't lump us together."

"No, no. Don't underestimate him," Sabu said, suddenly turning serious. "That man might be a nincompoop, but he's also this shop's savior."

"Savior?" I replied, my eyes getting wide.

"That's right. Ask him sometime." As he spoke, Sabu gave me a knowing look. Then to show off a bit, he said, "Adios," gave a little wave goodbye, and left the store.

Who cares, I thought. I have zero interest in whether my uncle thinks he's a savior or not. All I want is to go back upstairs and get under the covers and sleep.

Still, even I was amazed at how sleepy I was. I told Sabu that I was sleeping thirteen hours a day, but on days when the shop was closed, I slept all day long. I slept and slept and wished I could sleep forever. In my dreams, I didn't have to think of those awful things. My dreams were like the finest, sweetest honey. And I was like a honeybee, flying in search of more.

In contrast, there was nothing good about the hours I was awake. Even though I hated him, I was constantly thinking of Hideaki. The way he laughed. The way he touched my hair. I like everything about him: the way he was a little self-centered, the way he had a complex about being tone deaf, the way he cried so easily. I knew I was being an idiot, but when he and I were together, I truly was happy, and those memories were engraved into the cells of my brain so deeply I couldn't erase them.

Sometimes I even imagined that the words he said to me the last time were all lies. That he was just teasing me. "It's all fake," he'd tell me. He'd just wanted to play a little joke on me. And, of course, that wasn't true. If it had been true, I wouldn't be here.

So to put it out of my mind, and stop remembering what happened, I went on sleeping, perhaps out of stubbornness, perhaps for some other reason.

The time passed by so quickly that I could never catch up.

4

"Takako, you still up?"

One night at the end of summer, my uncle called out to me from the other side of the sliding door. When I looked at the clock, I saw it was eight o'clock—closing time for the bookshop.

"I'm sleeping," I said from under the covers.

"Come on. People who are sleeping can't answer back like that."

"But I am sleeping. Because I'm a—what'd you call me?—a sleep monster, remember?"

I heard him laugh through the door.

"Are you angry?" he said. "I talked to Sabu."

"I am angry. You said I was like a monster."

"Well, I was worried about you, so I talked to him. He's worried about you too. Come on, don't you want to go outside? There's a place I want to take you. How about it?"

"I'm fine," I replied, facing the sliding door.

But my uncle persisted. "Trust me, you won't regret it. And then I promise I won't interfere anymore with your sleeping."

"For real?" I asked warily.

"Pinky swear. If I'm lying, you can hit me three hundred times."

"That's a promise." When I glared at him through the little gap in the sliding door, I saw him smiling and nodding.

"I promise."

The place he wanted to take me was just a stone's throw from the Morisaki Bookshop.

"We're here!" he said, coming to a halt in front of a storefront on a little backstreet. It was an old wooden coffee shop that I didn't think I'd ever noticed before. An extremely elegant, middle-aged man with a mustache seemed to be the man in charge.

The name of the coffee shop, Saveur, lit up by the sign, seemed to float above the dark haze.

"This is my spot," he said. As soon as my uncle heaved open the heavy door, we could smell the rich aroma of coffee.

The man pouring boiling water into a special siphon placed on the counter greeted us as we came in.

"Hey, this is my niece, Takako."

I took a seat next to my uncle at the small counter and gave a quick bow.

Even without the mustache, the owner's slender, refined face would have been quite dignified. He was probably in his late forties. I wished my uncle, who looked like a kid no matter how old he got, would follow his example.

"A blend for me. How about you, Takako?"

"Um, me too."

I turned and looked around inside. It felt so peaceful there. The interior was lit by soft lanterns. Gentle piano music was playing. The blackened brick wall was covered with doodles and graffiti from past customers. All of it fit together beautifully and matched the warm, soothing ambience of the coffee shop. It's so nice here, I thought. For the first time in a long time, I felt joy well up inside me. And I felt a little bit better, a little less tired.

"This place has been around for fifty years," my uncle explained. "In the old days, a lot of famous people used to come here."

"Wow. I'm sure it wasn't easy to create an atmosphere like this," I said, nodding deeply. "It's so calming."

Around five minutes later, a waitress brought us our coffee.

"Good evening, Mr. Morisaki."

"Hey, Tomo, this is my niece, Takako."

"Nice to meet you," I said, bowing.

Tomo smiled and said hello.

"Tomo's one of our regular customers," my uncle said. "She's a true reader."

"Oh, I'm nothing special," she said, smiling shyly. She was about my age, maybe a little younger. She had fair skin and round, full cheeks. There was something gentle about her way of speaking. And she looked cute in her black apron. I had a feeling we might get along. My mood brightened.

"What's the deal, Takako? You prefer girls? There are young guys here too." My uncle waved to the other end of the counter. "Hey, Takano!"

A tall, thin young man promptly popped his head through a gap in the curtain from the kitchen.

"Takano! Why don't you take my niece out on a date sometime?"

"Hey!" I shouted and slapped my uncle's hand.

Takano seemed pretty shy. That's all it took for his face to turn completely red.

"Takano has been training here so he can open his own café someday. But all he does is screw up, so the owner's constantly yelling at him." My uncle looked genuinely happy as he said the part about being yelled at.

"Let's not start tarnishing his reputation," the owner interjected.

I felt bad for Takano, but he looked so unsteady on his feet that you could knock him over with a little push. He ended up inadvertently confirming what my uncle had said.

My uncle was still in a good mood afterward. A middle-aged woman sitting nearby called out, "Hey, Satoru!"

"Oh, Mrs. Shibamoto!" he said and went over to her with his tail wagging. Then someone else at another table called out his name, and he quickly moved over to them.

At the bookshop, my uncle kept things more under control, but take one step outside and he was totally different. I sighed, feeling like a dog owner being dragged around by her pet.

"Satoru's a popular guy around here." The café owner laughed wryly. When he smiled, the wrinkles around his eyes made him look kind.

"He's very friendly, if nothing else," I said, sarcastically. "But this truly is the first time I've ever had coffee this good. And I love the feel of this place. It's wonderful."

The owner gave a soft laugh. "Thank you very much. When young people come here for the first time, they see it with fresh eyes. That means a lot to me. It's Takako, right? Are you new to the area?"

"This is my first time. I just started living at my uncle's store."

"At the Morisaki Bookshop? That's a great spot. I really hope you enjoy life in Jimbocho."

I made a face and groaned a little.

"What's wrong?"

"My uncle says the same thing."

"That makes sense. No one loves this neighborhood more than your uncle."

I groaned again. "I'm not sure I get it. But I wasn't lying when I said your café was wonderful. I definitely want to come back."

"Anytime," he said and gave me a big smile.

We stayed so long at the café that when we left it was late in the evening. My uncle and I strolled around the neighborhood, just wandering. The night breeze was cool against my face. It already felt like autumn.

My uncle seemed drunk from the one beer he'd ordered. He walked ahead of me, stumbling a little and mumbling about what a nice night it was.

I realized then that it was the first time we'd gone for a walk together like this since my childhood. Back then, we would walk all day long near my grandfather's house, hand in hand, pretending we were exploring. Why was that so much fun? I was always giggling with excitement.

In those days my uncle always seemed more like a sweet older brother. I guess it's natural for an only child, especially one like me, so wrapped up in her own thoughts, to be so excited to be spending time with someone like that.

As my mind drifted back to that time, vivid memories returned to me . . . the two of us in his messy little room, him playing Beatles songs terribly on the guitar, and both of us singing . . . or spending hours reading Osamu Tezuka and Shotaro Ishinomori, totally engrossed in manga.

These memories made me start to feel a little bit of that same closeness to my uncle again as he walked ahead of me.

"Uncle Satoru?" His back was to me when I called out to him.

"Yeah?" My uncle turned and stared at me with those boyish eyes.

"What were you doing when you were my age?"

"I guess I just read all the time."

"That's all?" I felt a little disappointed. "That doesn't seem that very different from now."

"That plus traveling."

"Traveling?"

"Yeah, I would work a little here in Japan, save up some money, that kind of thing. Then I'd backpack around. I went to all kinds of places—Thailand, Laos, Vietnam, India, Nepal. I even went across Europe."

The idea that my uncle had been so adventurous amazed me.

"What made you want to do that? Didn't you think about getting a regular job?"

"Hmmm . . ." He folded his arms and spoke slowly, as if he was thinking back on that period of his life. "The short version is I wanted to see the whole world for myself. I wanted to see the whole range of possibilities. Your life is yours. It doesn't belong to anyone else. I wanted to know what it would mean to live life on my own terms."

I found myself nodding, but it seemed like a bit of a contradiction to escape Japan and go off in search of the possibilities for your life only to end up running the bookstore.

Still, listening to him talk, I realized just how different he was from the image of him I'd been holding on to since childhood. Now that I'm an adult, I think I can understand a little bit of what he felt then. In college, I used to dream about living a life that felt true to my own values, my own sense of things. Of course, when it came time to act on that in the real world, I found I just didn't have the courage.

That might have been the secret to why he was able to be so wild and free.

I felt a little jealous of him.

"Well, I guess I spent my twenties drifting around like that. My father was always getting angry at me. And then one day in the midst of all this, he dropped dead. And I ended up taking over the store for him."

"Do you regret it?"

"Not at all," he said, smiling. "There's no job that suits me better than this one. For someone who loves books, there's no place more wonderful than here. I'm proud to have a shop here. I can't thank my father and grandfather enough really."

"That's great."

"What is?" My uncle looked at me with a confused expression.

"That you're doing what you want, and you're making a living at it."

"That's not really true. I resisted it a lot in the beginning. I mean taking over the store from my father wasn't exactly what I dreamt of doing when I was young. Even now I still go back and forth all the time. But, I don't know, maybe it takes a long time to figure out what you're truly searching for. Maybe you spend your whole life just to figure out a small part of it."

"I don't know. I think maybe I've been wasting my time, just doing nothing."

"I don't think so. It's important to stand still sometimes. Think of it as a little rest in the long journey of your life. This is your harbor. And your boat is just dropping anchor here for a little while. And after you're well rested, you can set sail again."

"You're saying that now, but then you complain when I'm sleeping," I said spitefully.

He laughed. "Human beings are full of contradictions."

I was pouting without realizing it. Especially this guy, I thought.

"So, when you were traveling around and reading all those books, you must have learned a lot, right?"

"It's funny. No matter where you go, or how many books you read, you still know nothing, you haven't seen anything. And that's life. We live our lives trying to find our way. It's like that Santōka Taneda poem, the one that goes, 'On and on, in and in, and still the blue-green mountains.'"

"Uncle?" I thought that this might be my opportunity to ask the question I'd been wanting to ask him all along.

"Yeah?"

"Why did Aunt Momoko leave?"

"Hmmm ... She and I have the same way of looking at things. It's what brought us together, and I think it's also the reason we split up. We met in the middle of the journey and we fell in love. But that doesn't mean we'll always be traveling together. At some point, everyone has to find their safe harbor. I'd always thought we'd make it to the end together. Unfortunately, that's not how it turned out."

"What was it like ... when it happened? Were you sad?"

He looked up at the thick clouds covering the sky. "Of course, it was sad, but ..."

"But?"

"But, no matter where she is and what she's doing now, I want her to be happy."

"Still . . ." I couldn't understand how he could feel that way. "Didn't she dump you and leave?"

"But Momoko's still the one woman in my life that I've truly loved. That fact will never change. And the memories I have of our time together, they're all still here in my heart. So, in that sense, I'm still in love with her."

I wanted to ask him why, but there was something so sad about the look of him from behind, so small under the street-light, that I decided I couldn't say anything more.

That night, for some reason, I couldn't get to sleep. I felt strangely agitated. Even in the middle of the night, I was still tossing and turning. I remained there on my futon for a long time, struggling. All of these thoughts were swirling together inside my head, filling it until I thought it might explode. They kept going around and around, these painful memories of the past, of my old life. They commandeered my mind.

This is terrible, I thought. I sat up suddenly. If I don't do something, I said to myself, I'm going to suffocate here. I thought I could maybe watch TV, but then I remembered that would mean rearranging those stacks of books again first. It was three in the morning. Nothing was open outside no matter where you went.

As I stared into the darkness, I wished I had a book to read . . . It would've at least been a way to pass the time.

That's when it hit me. Isn't this a bookstore? I was practically drowning in books. I'd completely forgotten their original purpose because up till then I'd only seen them as a hostile presence in the room.

I turned on the light and started rummaging around, searching for an interesting book. But I had absolutely no idea how to judge which ones might be interesting. They all just looked like musty old books. I was sure though that my uncle could have easily picked out some that he loved.

At a loss, I stood in front of a mountain-sized stack of books and closed my eyes. Then I reached out my hand and pulled out the first book that I touched. It was titled *Until the Death of the Girl*. The author was Saisei Murō. I had heard his name before in my modern lit class back in high school, but that was all I knew.

So there in that dim room, with only the light of a little lamp near my pillow, I burrowed under my covers and began to read. My hope was that the book would be boring enough that I would fall right asleep. But a funny thing happened. An hour later, I was totally absorbed in it. Sure, there were some passages where the writing was difficult, but the subject of the book was human psychology, which is universal.

The story centers around a man trying to start his life in Nezu. After spending his childhood in Kanazawa, he moves to Tokyo to follow his dream and become a poet. There he gets entangled in a relationship with a woman who is the lover of a friend and his half-sister. He's struggling in poverty with no way to support himself in Tokyo when he meets the girl in the title by chance. It's through his relationship with her that he starts to heal his wounded heart, however briefly.

The main character has grown up in difficult circumstances and has survived a depressing youth, but somehow the whole story is suffused with this quiet tenderness.

Little by little, I felt something wash over me, a feeling of peace that words can't express. If I had to explain it, I'd say it could only have come from the writer's fervent love for life.

When I looked up, I realized the night was fading, and the day was beginning to dawn. I read on, turning one page after another.

That day, when Uncle Satoru came around, I was still feeling excited.

Usually I hardly greeted him, so when I leapt to my feet, he looked back at me with wonder.

I had *Until the Death of the Girl* in my hand. "This book was good," I told him.

How did he react? All of a sudden, my uncle's face lit up—just like a kid who had gotten a wonderful birthday present.

"Really? You liked it?" My uncle was as excited as if it had happened to him.

"Yeah, it was amazing," I said. "I don't know how to describe it. It hit home." I was frustrated that I couldn't come up with a better word. "It hit home" couldn't begin to describe the complex things happening inside me.

"No way! It means so much to me to hear you say that. I'm overjoyed. But going straight to Murō Saisei, that's jumping into the deep end."

My uncle was so profoundly happy that it somehow made me happy too.

We talked about the book for a while. It was a joy to feel connected to someone I'd felt I had so little in common with. It thrilled me even if it was just with someone like my uncle—no, it thrilled me even more because it was someone like him.

It was as if, without realizing it, I had opened a door I had never known existed. That's exactly what it felt like.

From that moment on, I read relentlessly, one book after another. It was as if a love of reading had been sleeping somewhere deep inside me all this time, and then it suddenly sprang to life.

I read slowly, savoring each book one by one. I had all the time in the world then. And there was no danger I'd run out of books, no matter how much I read.

Kafū Nagai, Jun'ichirō Tanizaki, Osamu Dazai, Haruo Satō, Ryūnosuke Akutagawa, Kōji Uno . . . I read them voraciously, the authors whose names I knew but hadn't read, the ones whose names I'd never even heard of, any book that seemed interesting. And yet for all I read, I found book after book that I still wanted to read.

I'd never experienced anything like this before. It made me feel like I had been wasting my life until this moment.

I decided to stop sleeping all the time. It no longer seemed necessary. Instead of taking refuge in sleep after my uncle took over for me at the bookshop, I went to my room or to a café to read.

These old books held more history within their covers than

I'd ever imagined. That wasn't limited to the content of the book itself. In each volume, I discovered traces of the years that had gone by.

For example, on a page of Motojirō Kajii's *Landscapes of the Heart*, I came across this passage:

The act of seeing is no small thing. To see something is to be possessed by it. Sometimes it carries off a part of you, sometimes it's your whole soul.

At some point in the past, someone reading this book had felt moved to take a pen and draw a line under these words. It made me happy to think that because I had been moved by that same passage too, I was now connected to that stranger.

Another time, I happened to find a pressed flower someone had left as a bookmark. As I inhaled the scent of the long-ago-faded flower, I wondered about the person who had put it there. Who in the world was she? When did she live? What was she feeling?

It's only in secondhand books that you can savor encounters like this, connections that transcend time. And that's how I learned to love the secondhand bookstore that handled these books, our Morisaki Bookshop. I realized how precious a chance I'd been given, to be a part of that little place, where you can feel the quiet flow of time.

As a result, I became pretty knowledgeable about the writers we carried. Before I knew it, I had become close with our regulars too. When Sabu realized something was a little different about me, he revised his earlier impression of me. "Hey, Takako," he said, "you're getting into it, aren't you?"

There was one more change: I started taking walks around

the neighborhood. It was right about the time when the weather had turned properly cool, the perfect season for walking around.

Day by day, the leaves of the trees along the streets turned to gold. It delighted me to see how well the changing colors matched the slow transformation happening inside me.

As I walked around, I saw the neighborhood so differently from when I first arrived in Jimbocho. Now, the whole place felt like the setting for an adventure. It was exciting. In any case, there were so many places I wanted to stop and check out all along the avenues and backstreets. It had such a strong downtown feeling, this little section of secondhand bookstores and coffee shops and foreign bars. And yet despite all that, there was nothing about its atmosphere that was chaotic in a way I couldn't stand. The whole neighborhood felt distinctly calm.

This is where I finally realized that even though we call them all "bookstores," each store has its own totally distinct flavor.

They're divided by their various specialties: some sell only novels, some only foreign literature, or historical novels. There were even shops that dealt only in film magazines, or children's books, or Edo-era texts bound in the traditional style. There were all kinds of store owners too. Some were stubborn old guys like my uncle, but there were also younger ones with gentler dispositions. I stopped by the welcome center one day, and they told me there were actually more than 170 bookstores here. Like my uncle said, it really was the world's greatest neighborhood for bookstores.

When at last I was tired from walking, I would stop at a coffee shop to rest. The warm coffee was perfect for the chilly season. Drinking a cup at the end of my walk, I felt relaxed to my core.

I *spent day* after day this way as we went deeper into autumn. I have no doubt that my new routine helped brighten my mood.

Things were still knotted up inside me, but it felt like the more I walked, the more they loosened up.

Perhaps, as a result, it was at that time that I started to get to know more people around the neighborhood. I became a regular at the Saveur coffee shop and started to get very close with the owner and the staff, especially with Tomo, the waitress.

Tomo was a first-year grad student in Japanese literature who was working at the Saveur in her free time. And sometimes she came to the Morisaki Bookshop as a customer. Two years younger than I was, she looked quiet and reserved, but deep down she was fiercely passionate. As you might expect of a grad student in literature, she had an incomparable love of writers. That wealth of knowledge was one of the things I admired about her.

Around this time, Tomo started coming by the store on her way home from work, even when she wasn't looking to buy anything, and the two of us would go to my room on the second floor and have tea together, surrounded by books.

The first time she came into my room, she lit up. "This place is amazing. It's like a dream."

"Really? It's so small—and there's no gas range." Since I was the one actually living there, I gave her my candid opinion. At least when it came to convenience, the place really had nothing to recommend it.

"Are those things really that important?" Tomo said, looking like I was the one who didn't get it. "Not a single thing here is superfluous. You reach out your hand and the books are right there. Isn't that wonderful?"

"I guess so."

"It's true," she said as she brought her face close to mine. Her eyes shone.

I looked around the room again. It was strange—somehow

her excitement about my room transformed the place from being dull into something wonderful. She suggested that we could make the room even nicer by buying some flowers at the corner florist. We arranged cosmos stems in a vase and placed it on the low table. The room felt so much brighter afterward. From that point on, I always decorated that spot with an arrangement of seasonal flowers.

One day as we were really becoming close, we were drinking tea together and I suddenly decided to ask her something.

"Tomo, how did you get so into books?"

She answered me in that same gentle voice. "That's a good question. When I was in middle school, I was painfully shy. I had this fear of telling people what I thought. And because of that there were just these terrible feelings rumbling around inside me. I was carrying around this awful shame. That's when I read the copy of Osamu Dazai's *Schoolgirl*. That's how it started for me. Now I'm basically totally addicted to reading."

"I think every serious reader at some point in their life encounters a book like that. And they never forget the experience," I said with admiration.

"Here's hoping we both encounter some wonderful books in the future," Tomo said with a smile.

"I hope so," I said, agreeing with all my heart.

Afterward, something else happened connected to Tomo.

Early one afternoon when I was tending the shop by myself, Takano, who worked at the Saveur, came by. I hadn't had many chances to talk to him because he worked in the kitchen, but it was hard to miss his lanky figure inside the shop.

I noticed him right away and said hello.

Takano bowed and greeted me, but he seemed restless as he wandered the shop looking around.

What an odd guy, I thought. "Anything in particular you're looking for today?" I asked.

"No, I'm, um . . . not . . ." he muttered incoherently.

What's going on with this guy? I wondered. His face was all red. He was acting just like a little boy in front of the girl he had a crush on. That's when it hit me. What if he was interested in me? I remembered that when my uncle had told him to take me out on a date, he'd gotten extremely embarrassed. As I thought it through, I found myself suddenly getting nervous too.

The awkward silence inside the shop dragged on for a while. The air seemed to get so thick with it that it was getting harder to breathe.

When I couldn't bear it any longer, I opened my mouth to say something, but at that very moment, he said in a loud voice, "Um!"

I braced myself automatically. I assumed he was about to confess his love for me, and so my mind was racing, wondering how I could delicately turn him down.

But what he actually said next wasn't what I was expecting at all.

"Does Miss Aihara come here a lot?" Takano's face turned bright red as he spoke.

"By Miss Aihara, you mean Tomo?"

"That's right."

"She often pops in during her lunch break from the coffee shop."

"What do you two talk about?"

At this point, my fever broke, and my anxiety subsided.

"Wait, do you have a crush on Tomo?" I asked.

"No, it's not that. It's just . . ."

"It's fine. I mean Tomo is really cute. But since you two work together, I'd think you might know her better than I do."

"No. I'm in the kitchen. She's in the dining area. And I'm terrible at talking to people."

"So it seems. You really are shy, aren't you?"

"Does she have a boyfriend?"

The tone of his voice as Takano asked the question suggested this was a matter of the greatest urgency.

"Well, now that you mention it, I've never asked her. But Tomo is a really cute, likable girl. I wouldn't be surprised if she did have a boyfriend."

"Would you be able to casually ask her for me?"

"Why would I be the one to ask her? Why don't you ask her yourself?"

"You two are good friends, Takako. You could ask her in a way that felt natural, right? And besides, I've never talked like that to a girl before."

"You're talking to me right now," I said, rather taken aback. Didn't I count as a woman? But Takano didn't seem to notice my reaction.

"I'm not asking you to do this for nothing. If you agree to help, anytime you come into the coffee shop, I'll pay for your coffee refills."

And with that, I wrote off all of his many offenses. My face lit up. "Really?" I asked. "In that case, I'll come every day."

"Every day? That might be a bit much . . ."

"Why do you sound so stingy? You'll be getting close to the woman you've been longing for, all for the mere price of a cup of coffee!"

"Ah . . ." Takano nodded reluctantly in approval. "But please promise me you won't mention a word of any of this to her."

"Understood," I told him, thumping my chest.

And that's how Takano and I entered into our secret agreement.

I learned that he had secretly been in love with her for half a year already. But in all that time, apparently, he hadn't done more than say hello to her. He'd spent the whole time off in the shadows thinking to himself how wonderful she was. That might sound weird, but you could also see it as innocent.

Having taken on this role, I wanted to try to make things work between them if at all possible. Tomo might think it was none of my business, but Takano seemed like a respectable young man, albeit rather shy and awkward. If I gave them a chance, I thought, it might not be a total bust.

So I worked hard, not for the free coffee, but for the good of those two young people. The first step was to gather some information on the sly. I came to learn that there was no boyfriend at present, and, it seemed, there was no one in particular that she had on her mind. Her favorite color was Prussian blue. Her favorite animal, the dormouse. And her favorite neighborhood was, naturally, Jimbocho. All of this seemed perfectly in line with what I knew of her, but it felt a little bit creepy that Tomo didn't know what was really going on.

Having obtained this new information, I proceeded to the Saveur, where I passed it along to Takano over a cup of free coffee. I leaned over the counter and whispered, "It looks like Tomo's favorite animal is the dormouse."

"That . . . that's amazing," Takano whispered back. Unfortunately, this led to the surprisingly nosy owner starting the false rumor among the regular customers that Takano and I were together.

What's more, all my hard work on behalf of our young couple proved totally useless. Takano, whose role was crucial, was not making any attempt to start a conversation with Tomo, which meant we were making no progress at all. He'd let out a victory cry when he learned she didn't have a boyfriend, but at this rate, it was going to take a decade before he could even start making small talk with her. It would all come to nothing.

I was getting impatient myself. There had to be some way to get these two talking. I thought of everything.

And then good news arrived from an unexpected source.

One afternoon, when Tomo and I were enjoying a quiet cup of tea, she told me about the used book festival.

"Used book festival? What's that?" I said, dumbfounded.

"You don't know about the festival, Takako? Every year in the fall, all the used bookstores in the area set up an outdoor bargain book market. So many people come, the whole neighborhood feels crowded and lively. It's incredible."

"Oh wow. That sounds fun."

"Your uncle's doing it too, of course."

"Really?"

"Yeah, all the stores join in."

I felt embarrassed that my uncle had never said a word about this major event. I vowed solemnly to exact my revenge on him later.

"I'm thinking about going this year," she said. "Do you want to walk around together?"

At that moment, I had a flash of inspiration. "Yes. Let's go. Let's go," I said, jumping at her offer. There might be a way to take advantage of this. I should tell Takano.

5

The Kanda Used Book Festival took place over the course of a week in late October. And for that week, carts and bookshelves, crammed with used books, crowded the streets in an open-air flea market.

The festival was such a success that it surprised me. Book lovers of all ages flocked to the neighborhood. Maybe because it was a once-a-year event, but the turnout went far beyond my expectations. You could feel the energy on Yasukuni and Sakura Streets. This old sepia-toned neighborhood of secondhand bookshops was now buzzing with activity before noon. It was a pretty spectacular sight.

Our Morisaki Bookshop joined in too, of course. My uncle and I brought out the cart with all the used books we'd set aside over the previous few days. To our delight, we had twice as many customers as usual come to the shop. There was even a brave soul who was so worried he'd miss out on the sale that he bought a whole cardboard box of our bargain books.

As expected, my festival-loving uncle was very much in his element. Apparently, he'd been coming to the festival almost every year since he was a kid. Thanks to that, he could feel his body start to ache in anticipation when that time of year came around.

"After this, it'll get cold, and the number of people coming to the store will decrease significantly," he said. "We need to make enough money now to get us through." It was rare for my uncle to talk like a businessman, but despite what he said, when I lost sight of him for a moment, he was off visiting other shops. Of course, it was up to me to bring him back.

On the evening of the third day, I ended work early with my uncle's permission and went out with Tomo to have a look around the rest of the festival. And who should appear then, apparently by accident, but Takano—just as we'd planned.

"Oh, what a surprise," he said.

"Oh, wow, it really is," I replied. We were lousy actors putting on an obvious charade, but Tomo was so innocent that she didn't seem to notice at all.

And, with that, one of us said, "The three of us should walk around together."

In front of Tomo, Takano was stiff and tense at first. I whispered to him discreetly, "What are you doing? You look like RoboCop."

"I've forgotten how to walk," he replied. Even his voice sounded robotic. Tomo overheard him and burst out laughing.

Why was it that all the excitement in the neighborhood seemed to lift our spirits as we walked around? The two of them were waltzing around with such animated expressions on their faces that they looked like a couple. Though at least in Takano's case, there was another major reason for this. When Tomo spoke to him, he looked ecstatic, like he was running through a field of flowers. The look on his face was so funny that I struggled not to burst out laughing.

We bumped into Sabu as we were rummaging through the books at the special booth set up at the main Jimbocho intersection. Sabu was with his wife, and he was holding so many paper bags that he could barely carry them in his hands. Sabu's wife looked so elegant in her perfectly matched kimono that I thought she might be too good for him. But seeing the two of them side by side, I could sense that they had the kind of bond that can only come from years spent together in good times and in bad. The feeling was overwhelming.

"It looks like you've bought quite a lot again," I said to Sabu when I saw all the bags he was holding.

"He has," his wife said mournfully, giving Sabu a little push from the side. "He keeps on buying more books. Our house is overrun with them right now. Would you mind coming by one day and buying all of them?"

"Oh no, please not that," Sabu said, panicking. "Didn't I downsize a bit the other day?" He put his hands together, begging her.

Even after they walked away, we couldn't stop laughing.

The crowds on Yasukuni Street didn't go away once it got dark. We were still happily walking around. We were on a shopping spree, buying all the books we could get our hands on. "There's an interesting shop over here," Tomo said, and took us to Kintoto Books, which sold grade-school textbooks from the Taishō era, in the early twentieth century. On a whim, I bought a Japanese textbook that cost two thousand yen. The language in it was so old that it ended up feeling surprisingly fresh.

In the evening as all the stores started to close, we went to the Western-style restaurant inside Sanseidō and ate dinner. By this point, Takano was pretty relaxed. He no longer seemed to see himself in a field of flowers every time he was in front of Tomo. It turned out he knew a lot about foreign literature. While we ate, he spoke so easily about the charms of Faulkner, Capote, and Updike that you never would have believed how awkward he'd been earlier. Tomo and I were both properly impressed.

In the end, it turned out to be a fulfilling and exciting day. Afterward, Takano thanked me and said how incredibly grateful he was, but I didn't see any reason to thank me, because I was the one who enjoyed it the most.

6

On the last night of the festival, after we closed the shop, I was sitting alone in my room in a daze. Outside the window, the streets were so quiet and still that the crowds of the past week already seemed like a dream. As I lay on my futon, the ticking of my alarm clock seemed too loud. I was staring up at the ceiling when I felt that strange uneasy feeling return, that loneliness I'd felt when I first arrived here.

Suddenly, there was a knock at the door. I felt my shoulders trembling. As I turned timidly toward it, I saw in the narrow opening at the edge of the sliding door an eye glaring back at me.

"Aahhhh!" I turned pale and shrieked like a heroine in a horror movie.

"Oh, did I surprise you?" a strange, high-pitched voice said. And then a shaggy head popped into view.

I heaved a sigh of relief.

"Please don't surprise me like that, Uncle."

"Sorry, sorry." He put down the plastic bag he'd been holding in both hands and said, "Mind if I come in for a second?" as he walked into the room. He took out some bottles of alcohol and juice and set them up on the little dining table. He'd even brought potato chips and shredded squid snacks.

"Didn't you go to the end-of-festival wrap party?" I asked.

"I just went to say hello and then I came back. Besides, I'd rather have a wrap party with just the two of us," he said with a smile like a mischievous child.

"Now that you mention it, we've never had a drink together."

"Well, okay, then. Let's do it." My uncle spread out all the contents of his plastic bag and we had our little wrap party. We sipped our sake, listening to the faint chirping of crickets through the open window. The quiet night enveloped us. Time passed so slowly that it felt like it had come to a halt.

My uncle stretched his legs comfortably as he leaned back against the bookshelf.

"Takako, it looks like you've totally gotten used to life here," he said.

"I think so too. At first I wasn't so sure it would work out, but somehow it has. I'm fully enjoying this little vacation from my life," I said with a little laugh.

"I'm glad to hear it."

"But I'm frustrated too."

"About what?"

"You knew from the beginning that I'd totally love it here."

"Don't feel bad about that. It makes me very happy that you like it. If you want, you know, you can stay here forever."

Hearing my uncle's kind words, I felt a little twinge in my heart.

"Why are you so good to me though? I know I'm your niece, but we hadn't seen each other in so long."

"Because I love you, Takako." He said it without any hint of embarrassment. He seemed almost distracted. "I know, for you, I might be some relative you don't know that well, but for me it's different. For me, you're an angel."

I almost spit out my beer.

No one had ever said anything like that to me before—no man, no woman had ever talked to me like that before.

"That's right. An angel. You're the person who saved me."

"Saved you?" I asked, understanding him less and less.

I had no memory of having ever done anything for him.

"That's right. You saved me. That's just my way of thinking of it. But I'm sure it won't be a very interesting story to you. Let's drop the subject."

"No, I want to hear it," I said sincerely.

My uncle stared at me for a moment and then asked if I promised I wouldn't laugh.

I nodded in agreement, and my uncle started speaking slowly, as if he were remembering something from long ago.

"It started in my late teens. I was feeling depressed. I couldn't see the value of life anymore. I couldn't seem to fit in, at home or at school. I just withdrew into myself and closed everything else out. I was overly self-conscious, I had too many ideals and ambitions for one person, and because of that, I ended up without a single one I could hold on to. I was an empty person. That's what I was. It seemed like there was absolutely nowhere I belonged in this world."

I'd never had the slightest inkling that my uncle had felt this way. But I also had no idea what on earth this had to do with me being an angel.

"You were born right around that time. I first met you when my sister brought you back home to introduce my father and everyone to his new granddaughter. The instant I saw you, so tiny wrapped up in your blanket, sleeping so peacefully, I thought I might cry. How can I put it? I could feel the mystery of life filling my heart. The idea of this child growing up, experiencing so many things for the first time, absorbing so much—all of it brought me as much joy as if it were happening to me.

"All of a sudden, I felt as if my twisted heart was being filled with warm light. It was still blurry, but I could feel a sense of purpose growing within me. That's when I made my decision. It was time to stop shutting myself up in a cage. It was time to get moving, to look around, and learn what I could from it all. Time to go in search of a place where I belonged, a place where I could say with confidence that I felt right. All the trips I went on, all the books I read, were the consequences of that decision. In other words, Takako, meeting you led me to a kind of epiphany."

"An epiphany . . . That's amazing."

"So, that's what I mean when I say you're the one who saved me. That's why I'll do anything for you."

My uncle said this so earnestly that I didn't know how to respond. I felt embarrassed by how childish I'd been, getting angry at him, and feeling sorry for myself. To think that all this time he'd cared so much about me. I felt like I finally understood the reason that he'd been so kind to me when I was little. I was an idiot. At the time I thought it was my natural right to be treated so kindly.

The joy of realizing that someone loved me that much made my heart want to burst. I tried to make a joke to hold back the tears welling up in my eyes. "Uncle," I said, "that's not exactly dialogue you should deliver while you're eating shredded squid."

My uncle laughed out loud.

"So did you end up finding the place you belonged?"

"Well, I guess you might say that. But it took me many years to get there." My uncle nodded quietly. "This is it. Our little, run-down Morisaki Bookshop. I had so many aspirations. I flew all over the world only to end up back at the place I'd known every bit of since I was a child. Hilarious, isn't it? After all that time, I came back here. That's when I finally realized it wasn't just a question of where I was. It was about something inside me. No matter where I went, no matter who I was with, if I could be honest with myself, then that was where I belonged. By the time I realized that, half my life was over. So I went back to my favorite harbor, and I decided to drop anchor. For me, this is a sacred place. It's where I feel most at ease."

"That reminds me," I said. "A long time ago, Sabu told me that you were the store's savior."

He laughed. "Its savior? That's a pretty big exaggeration. Basically, when my father fell ill, the business was on the brink—all I did was take over and keep it going. At first, my father was pretty strongly opposed to me taking over the shop. It was a tough time in the used book business, after all, and I was this irresponsible guy. But I got down on my knees and pleaded with him to entrust the shop to me."

"So that's how it happened."

"I mean I couldn't sit back and let it all fall apart, could I? This was where I spent most of my childhood. I would sit at the counter next to my father, quietly reading books like *Hans Christian Andersen's Fairy Tales*, and from time to time, he would stroke my head firmly with his giant hand. I was truly happy then. It felt like if this place was gone, then all of my memories would disappear too. I couldn't handle that."

I felt absolutely bowled over by what my uncle was telling me.

I'd thought I knew—or at least I'd meant to find out—what my relationship with my uncle was all about. Didn't I realize that he had his own private worries and pain? Didn't I see that his heart had been crying out for far longer than mine had? Why didn't I see how much was going on inside him?

Maybe the reason my uncle was always clowning around in front of people was to hide what he was feeling from them. The effort must have been excruciating. To look at him, they'd never realize what he felt inside . . .

The thought of it made my heart ache.

"I wish this place could have meant as much to Momoko too. She left just as I was trying so hard to rebuild the business. Right up until the end, I still had no sense what she was feeling beneath the surface."

"Uncle."

"Yes?"

"I love this shop. I really do."

I'd meant to say something more clever, but that was all that came out of my mouth. It was true, though, and I felt it sincerely.

"Thank you. This shop might not be indispensable for most people, but if it matters that much to even just one other person, then I feel I can keep it going for decades. It's like the line from Naoe Kinoshita in *Confessions of a Husband*, 'My boat travels lightly, drifting aimlessly at the mercy of the current.' That's how I want to live my life with this shop," my uncle said, and then he smiled without saying any more.

From that night, I started to think more seriously about my own life. I'd found a warm, calm place to stay here, but I couldn't remain dependent on others forever. If I did, I would never grow up. My heart would always be weak. I was convinced that if I didn't leave, I would never be able to start over.

But the moment I thought that, my fears came rushing back. The thought of leaving frightened me. *Just let me stay a little longer.* In my heart I was still dependent on others.

In the end, I hesitated, and, for a long time afterward, I went on living on the second floor of the Morisaki Bookshop.

Maybe I was waiting for some kind of cue. Then one day, suddenly, it arrived.

7

The call came on the second of January.

Instead of going home for the holidays, I spent the period around New Year's Day hanging around the bookshop. With the store closed until the fifth and my uncle off on a trip to the hot springs with his friends from the booksellers' association, I was all by myself.

Over the holiday, Jimbocho was a ghost town. Since there weren't any homes in the area, and the restaurants and companies were closed for the holidays, there was really no one around. There weren't even many cars driving down Yasukuni Street.

On New Year's Eve, Tomo and I went to visit the Yushima Tenjin Shrine, but besides that, my calendar was basically blank. So on New Year's Day and the day after, I got up early and strolled around the neighborhood. It felt great to walk around the deserted city. Even the air seemed much clearer. With my scarf fluttering in the wind, I made my way at random, stopping again and again to take another deep breath.

When I came home in the evening on the second, there was a blinking light on the cell phone that I'd left in the room. I'd already deleted the number from my phone, but I recognized it as soon as I saw it in my missed calls. At that moment, all of the good feelings of the day magically vanished. I felt my chest tighten. My finger trembled as I tapped the button and listened to the message.

"Hey, Takako, it's been a while. You good? I've got zero plans at the moment. You want to come out? If you call me, I can be right over."

I pressed delete before I'd heard the whole message. But it was too late. That awful feeling was already spreading rapidly through my heart. It happened so quickly. And now I would never get rid of that feeling.

When the shop reopened after the holidays, the pain in my heart only got worse. I can't put it into words exactly, but it was like there was this thing that was heavy and cold and it was starting to close around my heart. It made me realize once again that none of those things had ever been resolved. I had just tossed it all aside, waiting for my memories to fade away over time. But even though six months had gone by, just hearing his voice for a moment had left me all churned up inside. I understood at last that none of my problems had been solved. The trouble was still there.

"Takako, is there something you need to get off your chest? If something's going on, talk to me." Around the end of January as we were closing up the shop, my uncle suddenly said this to me.

I was flustered. "How did you know?"

"What do you mean? It's obvious just looking at you. Your uncle's not blind," he said, almost sulking.

It was just childish. I'd been acting like everything was normal, but my uncle saw through the whole thing.

"You seemed like you were doing really well, so I wasn't worried about you before. But lately, you just seem really off. When I try to talk to you, it's like you're not there."

"That's true, I guess . . ."

"Yes, it's true. Well, I might not be up to the challenge, but if you talk to me you might feel a little better."

I hadn't planned on telling anyone about it, but hearing what my uncle said, I realized I was wrong. I'd wanted someone to ask

me about it. I'd wanted someone to console me. I'd wanted someone to take care of me. It amazed me how utterly pathetic I was,
but my uncle's words had wiped out my defenses.

As we sat together in my room drinking, I told him the whole
story. Outside a cold winter rain started to fall. We could hear the
patter of raindrops hitting the window.

"It's not a big deal," I said to preface the story, and as I told him
what happened, I realized that it actually wasn't a big deal after
all. I'd lost my boyfriend and I'd lost my job. That's it. Midway
through the story, it all seemed so insignificant that I couldn't
help but laugh. I fought through it and finished the story, and
once I did, I felt a little bit better.

The whole time my uncle just listened without uttering a
word, as he drank his whisky with unusual speed. Even when I
finally finished my story after an hour of halting and stuttering,
he didn't say anything for a long time. He stared at the glass in his
hand like he was thinking of something.

Then, at last, he drained the remaining alcohol from his glass
and said decisively, "All right, let's go make him apologize. We're
going to make him say, 'I'm sorry I hurt you. I'm a terrible person.'"

I was dumbfounded. This was a totally unexpected development.

"What? Now? It's already eleven."

"Doesn't matter." As he said this, my uncle got up and started
to go outside. I grabbed hold of his arm in a panic.

"It's okay. I was being stupid. I just wanted to tell someone
what happened. You're drunk, aren't you?"

"Nah, I'm not drunk. Well, maybe a little. But that's beside the
point. Aren't you mad, Takako? He took advantage of you."

"Yeah, I'm mad. I've been getting madder and madder, and I'm
still mad.

"That's why we're going. You need to get this off your chest. If not, the ghost of this thing will haunt you forever."

"Yes, but I'll be even more embarrassed if it turns into me acting like a little kid trying to bring in my parents when I get in a fight," I said, on the verge of tears.

"There's nothing to be embarrassed about!" My uncle shouted in a voice that seemed shockingly loud coming from someone so small. The sound of his voice reverberated in the little room. "There's nothing to be embarrassed about. You are my niece, and you matter to me. I already told you, didn't I? I really love you. So I can't allow this guy to get away with that. It's my own ego. I can't let it go."

"You keep contradicting yourself. And, in the end, it just comes down to your ego."

"That's why I'm going to get this off my chest. Even if you don't come with me, I'm still going. Tell me the address. I'm going to give him a beating."

A beating? This conversation was suddenly heading in a dangerous direction.

"Wa-wait a second. That's not going to end well. Someone will call the police. And he was on the rugby team in high school and college. If a string bean like you tries to beat him up, you'll end up getting beat up ten times worse."

"Th-that doesn't faze me," my uncle said, but he started to back away a little.

"Come on. Let's not do anything foolish. Let's go back to drinking," I said, forcing a smile as I tried to smooth things over.

"Don't run away from it, Takako," my uncle said, turning back to me with a terrible seriousness. "I'm with you. Don't run away."

My uncle looked at me fiercely. I could see the intensity in his eyes. For a few seconds, we just stared at each other.

He was right. I couldn't run away. If I did, nothing would change. Wasn't that obvious?

I bit down hard on my tongue.

"Okay, I get it. Let's go, Uncle."

My uncle nodded firmly.

By the time we arrived in front of his apartment, after forty minutes in a taxi, the rain was growing more and more intense. We got drenched as we ran to the entrance without an umbrella.

"This is it?"

My uncle had stopped in front of the door with the number 204 on it.

"Definitely," I replied. Old memories were stirring inside me.

Thinking back, I probably only came here two times while we were together. When we met at someone's place, it was always mine. The fact that I was only now realizing there was something weird about this arrangement proved how slow I was.

Raindrops dripping from his hair, my uncle rang the doorbell without a moment's hesitation. My whole body was trembling from the cold and the stress. I felt nauseous too. Whatever assertiveness I'd felt when I said "I get it" faded away quickly once I was standing in front of Hideaki's place.

As I stared at the metal door waiting for a response, deep down I thought about how much better I would feel if we just left and pretended nothing ever happened. But it was already too late. We heard someone rummaging around on the other side of the door, then the click of the door unlocking, after which the door opened about the width of a finger.

A low, familiar voice said, "Who is it?"

My uncle immediately grabbed the door and forced it open.

Hideaki was standing stock-still in the entrance, wearing a

tracksuit, his mouth open in shock. He had probably just fallen asleep. His hair was messy and you could see the imprint of his pillow on his cheek. But those solid, well-defined shoulders and almond-shaped eyes were just as I remembered them. It made sense, of course. It's not as if ten years had passed. In that moment, I felt that stabbing pain in my chest return.

Hideaki looked back and forth at the two of us, wide-eyed with surprise, then turned to my uncle and asked, "Who are you?"

"I'm Takako's uncle."

"Huh?"

"I'm her uncle Satoru. Her mom is my older sister."

"No, I get that part. I mean what are you doing here?"

"Oh, I wouldn't be here without a reason. Do we look like we're here to ask you to subscribe to a newspaper?"

"No, I mean, tell me what business you have here," Hideaki said, sounding a little exasperated.

I was watching the back-and-forth between them anxiously. My uncle was being extremely aggressive that night.

"You want to know why we're here? We're here because you did something terrible to her. Don't act like you have no idea what I'm talking about."

"Eh?" The volume of Hideaki's voice went up a level. But my uncle wasn't the least bit daunted.

"You toyed with her emotions so mercilessly that you drove her to quit her job. Don't you feel anything? Don't you feel any remorse for hurting someone so badly?"

"Hey, hey. I hurt her? Is that what she said?"

"That's right."

"Are you stupid? Maybe it's because you're her uncle, I don't know, but you think you can just swallow everything this woman says? It's obvious she's lying. She's the one who pushed herself on me!"

"How would she benefit from lying? Isn't it your fault that she quit her job, and that she's still suffering?"

"She probably quit because she felt like it."

My uncle let out a big sigh when he heard what Hideaki said. "It's no use, Takako. This guy's rotten to the core."

"Hey, old man, watch what you say."

Hideaki came forward into the hall, glaring at my uncle. My uncle was short, and Hideaki was so tall that there was an almost twenty-centimeter difference in height between them. So even though my uncle was glaring back at Hideaki, the impact was, unfortunately, limited.

"Is something wrong?"

A woman in pajamas poked her head out from inside the apartment. It was his fiancée, Murano.

Things had gone from bad to worse. Standing there might be embarrassing, it might be unbearable, but there was no way out now.

"Takako?" Murano said. When she noticed me, she frowned and said, "What on earth happened? You're all wet."

"She showed up out of nowhere. Isn't that right, Takako? Have you gone crazy? What were you thinking of showing up in the middle of the night with this old man in tow?"

"Tell him, Takako."

"Umm . . ."

Frightened, I looked and saw everyone was staring at me.

How had I ended up here?

I felt pierced by their glances. I wanted to disappear in a puff of smoke. They were all waiting silently for me to say something.

I ransacked my brain for something to say that might somehow bring the situation to a peaceful end.

I was just in the neighborhood and thought I'd drop by . . . I was hoping he'd return a book I'd lent him . . . I wanted to congratulate you on your engagement . . . No. That was all wrong. What I wanted to say was something else entirely. Why was I here? To get something off my chest. If I just told them what they wanted to hear, that wouldn't fix anything.

I told my heart to brace itself.

"I . . ."

Everyone's attention was focused on my mouth. I took a deep breath. My uncle was looking at me with encouragement. Tears formed in my eyes. And at that moment I could feel all of the emotions that had been building in my chest welling up within me. There was no time to think—suddenly, the words came pouring out of my mouth in a torrent.

"I came because I want you to apologize! You might have just been playing around, but it wasn't like that for me. I really loved you. I am a person. I have feelings. You might look at me and see just a woman you can take advantage of, but I think about things, I breathe, I cry. Do you know how much you hurt me? I . . . I . . ."

After that, I was at a loss for words. I was also sopping wet from head to toe from the rain and the tears and my runny nose. But after all this time, I had finally been able to say the words I'd wanted to say that night in the restaurant.

"Well said, Takako," my uncle said, putting his arm around me and drawing me close to him.

"What are you going to do? She just told you honestly how she feels. You have to respond."

Hideaki hung his head for a long time, saying nothing. Finally, he muttered quietly, "This is ridiculous. I don't have time to hang around with people like you who have nothing to do. I'm going to bed. Unless you want me to call the police, you'd better go home."

After he said this, he quietly closed the door. We could hear the lock click on the inside of the door. Then it was quiet in the hall.

"Hey!"

My uncle stared at the door with the intensity of a bullfighter. Then he banged on it loudly with his fists. I held on to him desperately from behind.

"That's enough, Uncle."

"But Takako."

"It was enough. Really. I feel better, maybe better than I've felt in my whole life up till now. It's amazing. This might be the first time I've ever raised my voice and told another person what I really felt," I said, and then burst out laughing at my uncle with my face covered in tears and snot.

"If you say so, Takako . . ." my uncle mumbled, seeming a little dissatisfied.

"It's really okay now."

"Let's go home then, shall we? At this rate, we'll both catch a cold."

Facing the door, I murmured a final goodbye to the place, and then I left it all behind.

In the taxi on the way home, we barely said anything. My uncle, having exhausted all his energy, lay slumped in the back seat. I sat beside him, set free at last from my anxieties, lost in my own thoughts.

It wasn't solely Hideaki's fault. I'd known that from the beginning. I was half to blame for the way things turned out. It was my carelessness and my lack of will that made the situation possible.

But I'd just needed to say what I was feeling, no matter what.

Even if someone told me I was being selfish, I had to share what I was thinking. I'd been suffering because I was too weak to do that. Maybe Hideaki never believed he had any reason to be blamed, and he felt caught off guard by my reaction, but I still needed to vent what I was feeling to him. If not, I couldn't move on. No matter how much time passed, I'd still be stuck. If my uncle hadn't given me the chance, I would've just been left holding on to these feelings forever.

I turned the words around inside my mind, trying to express how grateful I was to my uncle. But nothing came out. In the end, the only thing I could come up with was just one word. So I said it to him sincerely.

"Thanks . . ."

My uncle smiled and pulled me by the shoulder closer to him. Sensing the warmth of his body next to mine, I felt a wave of relief well up from deep within me.

I was protected. There was someone who worried about me, who got angry because what happened to me mattered as much as if it had happened to him.

For a long time, I'd let myself feel like I was totally alone in this big world, but all along there was someone close by, thinking about me, looking out for me. That made me immensely happy.

The taxi we were riding in drove silently across the rainy, neon-streaked city.

8

It was right after that that I decided to leave the shop. As strange as it might sound, that event gave me the boost I needed. All my troubles had vanished, and my body felt light. At last I was ready to leave.

I found a new place where I could live starting in March. It was pretty far away from the shop, but it was the best I could do. I still had a lot of questions about what I was going to do next. For the time being, however, I'd gotten a part-time position at a little design firm through my old job.

When I told my uncle I intended to leave, he seemed quite surprised. "You don't have to rush into any decisions," he said in a panic.

But I had already made my decision.

"I've been enjoying this little vacation from my life for a long time already. If I don't go now to look for the place where I belong, I might end up never finding it."

My uncle listened to me, but he didn't say anything else.

The month before I moved to my new place, I savored my last days at the Morisaki Bookshop. I worked diligently and spent my free time reading lots of books. Out of gratitude, I also did a deep clean of the shop and the second floor. And I even carefully organized the collection of books that was crammed haphazardly into the spare room on the day I arrived.

I let the regular customers and everyone at the Saveur know that I was leaving. They were all sorry to see me go. It almost made me cry to discover they cared so much about me. Sabu went so far as to say that I should marry his son and join his family. And it seemed like he was actually going to bring him by to set us up.

Takano and Tomo held a little going-away party for me. We gathered around a hotpot in my room on the second floor of the shop and celebrated late into the night. Tomo told me how sad she was that her book-loving friend wouldn't be around anymore. "Next year," she said, "let's go to the festival together again, okay?"

That night Takano whispered to me that he'd taken Tomo to the movies in Shibuya a bit earlier. They didn't seem to be a couple yet, but, given where Takano had started, this sounded like substantial progress. I was so happy to hear it, I actually said, "Not bad!" and slapped him as hard as I could on his slender back.

It was after this that Murano, Hideaki's fiancée, contacted me unexpectedly, and we met up at the coffee shop to talk. My biggest worry about that night was that we'd ended up being terribly rude to her as well. I headed to the place we'd agreed upon, planning to offer my sincere apology. But once we were face to face, she was the one bowing deeply to apologize to me. She said she'd had her suspicions about his behavior earlier on, but after my unusual appearance that night, everything clicked for her. She questioned him again and again until he finally confessed. Until that night, she said, she never would have guessed that I was the other woman.

I kept trying earnestly to apologize to her. I said, "I'm to blame too," but she just shook her head. She said the wedding was off now. When I heard that, I rushed to apologize again, but she said firmly, "It's not your fault, Takako."

That guilty feeling stayed with me though. When I told my uncle the next day what had happened, he said, "She's right. Isn't it better to find out now instead of after they're married when it's too late?" My uncle might be biased since he despised Hideaki, but when I realized he had a point, I felt a weight being lifted off my shoulders.

My uncle and I spent my last night at the shop drinking coffee together on the veranda on the second floor, staring up at the dark winter sky.

He gave me a giant stack of old books to remember my days at the bookshop. He said they were all books that had made a deep impression on him when he was young. Peeking into the heavy paper bag, I saw he'd filled it with books by some pretty serious writers, people like Takehiko Fukunaga and Kazuo Ozaki.

We spent our last night together feeling really at ease with one another. I'll never forget what my uncle said to me then.

"There's one thing I want you to promise me," he said first as a preamble. Then he said, "Don't be afraid to love someone. When you fall in love, I want you to fall in love all the way. Even if it ends in heartache, please don't live a lonely life without love. I've been so worried that because of what happened you'll give up on falling in love. Love is wonderful. I don't want you to forget that. Those memories of people you love, they never disappear. They go on warming your heart as long as you live. When you get old like me, you'll understand. How about it—can you promise me?"

"I get it. I promise," I said. "I think this place taught me that. So you don't have to worry."

"In that case, you'll be alright, no matter where you go."

"Thank you, Uncle."

The day of my departure, I stood in the morning light, staring at the Morisaki Bookshop. Such a tiny old wooden building. I lived here, I thought, but I could hardly believe it.

I remained where I was for a while, my breath turning white in the cold air. The street was enveloped in soft morning light. None of the stores had opened yet, and everything around seemed so profoundly peaceful and quiet.

I stood up straight, faced the shop, and bowed deeply. I vowed never to forget what my life at the bookshop had given me.

My uncle took the trouble to see me off despite how early it was. I thanked him from the bottom of my heart.

He had become an enormously important part of my life. It's funny. I never would've imagined things turning out this way when I first arrived here.

As we said goodbye, my uncle's manly attitude of the night before suddenly disappeared and he let himself sob like a child in front of everyone.

"I can't take it. Please don't go, Takako," he said, holding my hand so tightly I thought he might never let go.

"I can come back and see you anytime," I said. It seemed backward, but I was now consoling him.

"You take care of yourself for me, will you? And I'll look after the shop, no matter what."

It felt like if I stayed there a second longer, I'd lose my nerve to leave. So I quickly said goodbye to my uncle, who was still trying to hold on to me, and walked away down the street.

I kept on moving, making it to the end of Sakura Street without looking back. As I was walking, the memories came rushing back, and tears filled my eyes. But I somehow held on and walked to the end of the street.

Then on a hunch I stopped and snuck a look behind me. I saw my uncle standing right in the middle of the street waving to me, looking so small in the distance. Seeing him like that, I couldn't hold on any longer. I burst into tears and started to sob.

I waved back to him with my face crumpled, and tears came pouring down my cheeks.

In response, my uncle waved back even more enthusiastically. I could see the morning light shining behind him.

I shouted, "Take care!" turned around, and walked into the crowds of Yasukuni Street.

Seeing me sobbing as I marched down the street, the people I passed must have surely thought there was something wrong with this weird woman. But I didn't care in the slightest. After all, I was crying because I wanted to cry, and these were the happiest tears I'd ever known.

In the brisk early morning air, I sensed a faint sign of the spring to come. I looked straight ahead and kept going.

Part Two

Momoko Returns

1

"Takako, it's been so long! I feel like I've been away for a hundred years."

That's how my aunt Momoko greeted me when she saw me in front of the Morisaki Bookshop. She let out a loud laugh. She had a voice that carried, and you could hear it reverberating down the little street of bookstores.

It was true. She had come back. Now that she was standing in front of me, it finally felt real. Uncle Satoru had told me she was back and so I knew this, at least, in my head. But until I actually saw her, I didn't really believe it. If a friend had told me they'd seen a ghost, I would've felt the same way.

But Momoko was really there. And she was incredibly cheerful. What was she so cheerful about? Was this the behavior of someone who suddenly reappeared after disappearing for five years? Uncle Satoru, on the other hand, was standing there looking like a dog who had just eaten something rotten. Shouldn't it have been the other way around?

"You look like you've seen a ghost," she said to me, acting offended. "That's a little harsh." I hadn't said a word to her this whole time.

I almost told her I would've been less surprised if I had seen a ghost, but somehow I held back and managed to say, "You look great." It had been more than ten years since we'd seen each other.

When Momoko was young, she was quite pretty. Maybe not drop-dead gorgeous, but there was a quiet beauty to her that caught your eye in an odd way. Like a stone you see glittering on the beach that's not worth much on the market, but there's still something about the way it shines. When I was a child and I saw her at family gatherings, I was always impressed by the way she sat so properly, tucked away in the farthest corner, as if she were trying not to stand out (Momoko is pretty small in stature). There was something almost mystical about her.

Despite the years, Momoko was still beautiful. She wore a simple outfit—a brown sweater with blue jeans—and barely any makeup. And yet with her perfect posture, her expressive face, and her brisk way of talking, she still seemed young. Rather than getting older, she looked more like she'd shed anything that was unnecessary.

In any case, this woman who was bursting with energy didn't look at all like someone who had run off and suddenly come home. My uncle, on the other hand, with his hunched posture, shabby clothes, and messy hair, was looking awfully old.

"Takako, you look just like your mother," Momoko said, narrowing her eyes and squinting at me. "At your grandfather's funeral, you were in high school. It seems like that was just yesterday."

And that's how my uncle Satoru, my aunt Momoko, and I were all reunited on a bright and clear autumn evening, in front of the Morisaki Bookshop.

2

"She's back."

Two days earlier, my uncle had called. He sounded agitated. It had already been a year and a half since I'd left the Morisaki Bookshop.

After my long vacation there had ended, I started working at a small design firm. Three months ago, they'd promoted me from part-time to full-time, which meant that my days were slightly busier, so it had been about a couple of months since I'd stopped by for a visit.

So when my uncle called me, I'd assumed he was just going to ask me to come see him. But hearing how upset he sounded, I knew something big had happened.

On the phone, my uncle described the situation in so much detail that I started to get impatient. To briefly summarize our two-hour conversation, this is what happened.

On that particular day, my uncle had been working in his shop in Jimbocho from the morning to the evening, as usual. At lunch, he'd sold some rare volumes of Ōgai Mori and Sakunosuke Oda, a pretty good haul for the day, so he was in a particularly good mood at the start of the evening. He was whistling as he closed up the shop when he heard someone quietly open the front door and come inside.

He thought, "Oh no, a customer at this hour?" But he had his back to the door and was focused on closing for the day.

The customer didn't seem to be coming any farther inside. They were just standing there in front of the door, almost like they were holding their breath. How odd. My uncle started to get suspicious and turned around. Then he heard the customer mutter something. Hearing that voice was such a shock that my uncle said it felt like "getting hit over the head ten thousand times."

At first, he thought he must be wrong, but he knew there was no way that could be true. It was impossible for him not to recognize that voice—as impossible as squeezing a hundred people into the Morisaki Bookshop.

While my uncle was still frozen with his back to her, unable to move, the customer repeated what she'd said a little more clearly, "Satoru . . ."

He took a deep breath and turned at last to see the owner of that voice. Suddenly, the familiar interior of the store receded into the distance, and there, in focus in the center of his field of view, was a single figure: his wife, who had left him five years earlier without so much as a word, until this moment. He couldn't look away from her. He felt like he was dreaming. He'd had dreams like this hundreds of times before. But in those dreams, his wife had never felt this real. It was definitely Momoko standing there, looking almost exactly the way she did before she left.

After a long silence, Momoko quietly smiled and said, "I'm home."

She said it exactly as if she'd just come back from a short walk. Her only luggage was a little bag she held in one hand.

My uncle stared at her for a long time before he finally replied, "Welcome back."

Without saying anything more, Momoko went up quietly to the room on the second floor. She'd been living on the second floor of the bookshop ever since . . .

"Wait, wait, wait a second." I had been listening patiently on the phone, but at this point he had gone past the limits of my endurance.

"What!? What's all this *'I'm home!' 'Welcome back!'* What do you mean she moved in? It sounds like a ghost story."

"But it's all true, Takako," my uncle replied earnestly.

"If that's true, then you're both weird. Why did Momoko suddenly come back? And why did you just welcome her in without getting upset?"

"I don't understand it myself," my uncle said, sounding bewildered. He seemed deeply affected by what he'd told me. "But it happened so naturally."

I was now too flabbergasted to speak. Granted, my uncle was a pretty unusual person, but the way they both were acting flew in the face of common sense.

"And after that did she happen to tell you anything more?" I asked him in all seriousness.

My uncle replied nonchalantly, "Yeah, I don't know. It's kind of hard to ask about it."

"Well, in that case, why don't you take her back to the house in Kunitachi and ask her about it the right way?"

"She doesn't like it there. She says it's hard to relax. She likes it better on the second floor of the shop. Listen, Takako, I don't have the slightest idea how women's emotions work. Why do *you* think she came back?"

I could hear how perplexed he was at the other end of the

receiver. But I replied coldly, "How should I know? She's your wife. Shouldn't you know her better than anyone else?"

"I thought I knew her better than anyone else, but now everything's screwed up. I'm groping around in the dark. You're a girl. There's got to be some kind of mutual understanding you share as women, right?"

"We have the same gender, but I think we might be entirely different species," I said. My uncle was quiet for a long time, then he just said, "But, Takako . . . do you think . . . she's going to leave again?"

Hearing the urgency in my uncle's voice made me change my mind a tiny bit. I could still see how sad and lonely he'd looked from behind as he walked wearily up the road that night I asked him about Momoko. He still loved her, no matter what. And he was still in pain. I never wanted to see him like that again if there was anything I could do about it.

"You don't want her to go?"

"I don't know. Before, I used to think that as long as she was happy where she was, I was fine with that. But now she's back, my feelings are starting to change. But that doesn't mean that I want her to be unhappy. Ah, I'm such a jerk."

Good grief. We weren't going to make any progress this way. I gave up and asked him, "So, what do you want to ask me?"

"Huh? How did you know I wanted to ask you something?"

"I know. How much time have we spent together?"

"Ah, Takako, there's no more wonderful niece in this world. I owe you."

It was mostly what I expected, but my uncle wanted me to find out what Momoko was really thinking. Why had she come back now? And what did she plan to do next? He said that five years ago she'd left behind a two-line note: "I'm fine. Please don't look for me." She didn't really take any bags with her. Since he hadn't noticed any signs or advance warning that this was going to happen, he had no idea what was going to happen now.

He had mixed feelings about it, but after a lot of worrying, he ended up following the instructions in her note and didn't look for her. He said he never even put in a missing person's report to the police. "We were never blessed with children of our own," he said, "and she took a liking to you, Takako. That's why I think you're the one she'll talk to." He added, "Thanks in advance!" at the end before he hung up.

Aunt Momoko had taken a liking to me? Even though we'd barely ever talked? It seemed pretty doubtful. People tend to find it embarrassing when an outsider intrudes on their marital problems. But after hearing him pleading with me, there was no way I could turn down my uncle. After all, I owed him everything.

3

"Let's go inside," Momoko said. "We've got a lot to talk about."

At Momoko's urging, the three of us stopped standing in front of the shop and went in. I hadn't set foot inside the store in two months.

As usual, the shop was overflowing with books. When you walked, the wooden floorboards creaked beneath your feet. Dust drifted back and forth in the soft light of the setting sun streaming through the window. I took a deep breath and filled my lungs with that familiar scent.

I remembered the first time I walked into the shop—how my uncle laughed with embarrassment when I winced and said, "It smells musty." Strange that now I loved that musty scent of old books so much I couldn't get enough of it.

The three of us gathered around the counter, eating sweet tai-yaki cakes. I had picked them up on the way as a little gift. Twice while we were eating, customers came into the shop. They looked rather startled to see us huddled together like a bunch of mice, and bought their books. Momoko handled the customers for my uncle, talking to them in a friendly way. After so many years as the wife of a bookseller, she had plenty of experience.

After we went inside, Momoko still did nearly all of the talking. But it was impossible to follow the way she veered from one thing to the next. She was like a plane in a tailspin.

"Takako, you lived here once? That's just like me now, isn't it?

The AC doesn't work at all so summer here must've been hot. Oh, the sweet filling in this taiyaki cake goes all the way through! It's so good. Where'd you buy it? This neighborhood has changed since the old days. There are more fancy stores. Ugh, saying 'fancy' makes me sound so middle-aged, doesn't it?"

As she bounced from topic to topic, Momoko also, for some reason, occasionally reached out and pinched my uncle's cheeks. She had pinched him so many times that both of his cheeks were already bright red.

It seemed so strange and surprising to me that I interrupted her and said, "Um, why were you just pinching his cheek?"

"Oh, was I pinching them?" Momoko asked, looking surprised.

"You definitely were."

"It's just an old habit of mine, pinching people. When I feel close to someone, I just find myself pinching them. Maybe it's a way of showing affection. But wasn't Satoru's face kind of cute when I was pinching him?"

As she said this, Momoko pinched both of my uncle's cheeks firmly, moving them up and down and side to side, as if this were some punishment in a children's game. My uncle's face looked so incredibly miserable. It wasn't especially cute.

"Quit it . . ." My uncle cried out in pain, but he let her do it. He seemed used to it. You could hear in his voice that he had half resigned himself to it. His reaction made Momoko burst out laughing. Finally, she let him go. It seemed like Momoko had a hidden sadistic streak.

"Aren't you embarrassed to do that in front of Takako?"

"What's the big deal? She's not a total stranger. She's our niece."

"We're supposed to be adults. What about our dignity?" my uncle asked.

"Since when did you have any dignity?" Momoko hit back.

If she and I become close, am I going to end up getting pinched too? As I watched them banter, I shuddered at the thought.

Then Momoko jumped to another topic.

She suddenly grabbed hold of both my hands and fixed her gaze on me.

"But I'm so happy to see you. I used to think about you sometimes, you know. I'd wonder what had become of my sweet little niece. After all, you seemed like such a lovely young woman when you were in high school, so quiet and composed. And you looked so cute in your pageboy haircut."

"Is that what you thought of me? I really wasn't anything like that." I was at a loss for words. Back then I was at the peak of puberty; I always felt like I was about to be crushed under the weight of all my frustrations, all these feelings I couldn't express to others or process internally. I was in agony. It's hard to believe that someone could have seen me so differently. The only reason I was so well-behaved at family gatherings was simply to avoid drawing any attention to myself.

People's impressions really aren't very reliable, are they? That's what crossed my mind as Momoko was staring at me with a twinkle in her eye. I was wrong about so many things when it came to my uncle too. In the end, it doesn't matter if you're related by blood or if you spend years together in the same class at school or the same office; unless you really come face to face, you never really know someone at all. It was like that with Hideaki too. I couldn't avoid the fact that I bore a lot of responsibility for what happened. It made me start thinking about all that again.

"So, Aunt Momoko, I get the sense that maybe my old image

of you was pretty far off too," I countered with a touch of irony. But Momoko gave a hearty laugh as if she didn't mind at all.

"Well, at those family gatherings, I was playing the good girl too. Don't you think a lot of the people in that family are a bit stiff? My father-in-law was definitely one of them. Come on, his facial expression never changed. You'd think he was wearing a Noh mask. Plus the fact that we'd run off and gotten married. Those family get-togethers were unbearable. When we showed up, everything got so tense. That's why I was always tucked away in a corner, trying not to be noticed."

"So that's what it was like. And you still got married?"

"Well, we were living together at the time, so they still saw us as suspect. We met in Paris and fell in love, and as soon as we came back to Japan, they added my name to the family register. We just got caught up in the momentum, I guess."

"Pa-Paris?" I cried. "Why Paris?"

"You didn't know? I happened to be living in Paris then. He was traveling around on the cheap, and we used to run into each other sometimes at the used book stalls at the flea market. You'd think a guy from a family that owns a used bookshop wouldn't need to go to bookshops when he was off traveling. Not this guy. Plus he had this bushy beard and dressed in rags, so he looked like a beggar."

"That way you don't end up getting targeted by pickpockets and muggers," my uncle tried to explain, but Momoko didn't pay him any attention.

"But once I started talking to him, he turned out to be a pretty interesting guy. A little dark, maybe, and not sure what to do with himself. The kind of person who needed looking after. Then I ended up thinking I might hang out with him a little bit . . ."

"Oh, really?"

At some point, I started to catch on to Momoko's rapid narration. So the two of them met while my uncle was dealing with his issues by traveling around the world. Still, Paris was romantic. But what I couldn't understand most of all was why Momoko was in Paris. I tried asking her, but she only said, "Oh, I was young, you know," and did her best to dodge the question.

This woman is full of mysteries, I thought.

"Anyway, that's how we met. We came back to Japan, got married, and everyone gave us the cold shoulder, but then his father fell ill, and Satoru decided to take over for him. After that we worked together desperately to show them all up.

"It never occurred to me to try and show them up," my uncle interjected.

"Liar! You had all sorts of issues about your father! I figured that much out."

My uncle did not make a sound. He just sat there looking dejected. She was his wife, but he didn't seem to be much of a match for her. It was the first time I'd ever seen him like that; it was so funny I almost burst out laughing a few times.

And yet if you looked at it objectively, they actually seemed like a genuinely happy couple. As funny as it sounds, I even felt a little jealous of their relationship. The intimacy between them made them seem less like a married couple and more like old friends or comrades. It definitely put me at ease.

After a while, my uncle left, mumbling an excuse about how the store was busy, and Momoko pulled me upstairs to the room on the second floor. She suddenly leaned in close like she wanted to share something in secret.

"That's why I want us to be friends, Takako."

She took my hand and fixed her gaze on me again. Her hands were so small, I thought, like a child's.

"Ah ..."

"It's not fair that you're only close with Satoru. I want you and I to be close too. Does that sound good to you?"

"Ah ... yes ..." I nodded to her, but in my head I grumbled, *This isn't going to be easy.*

4

When night fell, I fought off Momoko's attempts to make me stay longer, said goodbye, and left the bookshop.

I wandered along the narrow backstreets on my way to the train station. The night was cool, with just a slight chill in the air. As I passed beneath the streetlights, the shadows I cast on the asphalt grew longer.

As I reached the Saveur, my feet stopped on their own. Seeing the orange light of its sign shining in the lonely street at night, I was like Pavlov's dog—it triggered a sudden urge to drink coffee. When I looked at my watch, it was just a little after eight. I opened the door. It was like something was pulling me inside.

The coffee shop was as lively as it always was, even at this time of night. From the entrance, I could hear the sound of gentle piano music mixed with the lively conversations of the other customers.

Then I spotted a familiar figure sitting at the counter. Seeing that short and stout body and smooth bald head from behind, I knew it could only be Sabu. He was deep in conversation with the owner about something or other. When he noticed me, he waved and called for me to come over and sit beside him.

The owner greeted me with his usual smile as I sat down next to Sabu. "Hey, Takako, it's good to see you back."

Just as I was about to smile at him, Sabu cut in, saying, "Takako, you've got to smile more. Try to be a little friendly. That's why you're not popular with the guys."

I told him it was none of his business.

Sabu giggled as if something were funny. "But you came at the right moment," he said. "We were just talking about all of you. Momoko came back, right? Satoru's playing it cool—why didn't he tell me about it?" You could hear the obvious curiosity in his voice.

"Sabu, let's not pry too much," the owner said, reprimanding him.

"Why? What's the big deal? Besides, aren't you the one who told me about it? You said Momoko had come back," Sabu said, pretending to sulk. There's absolutely nothing cute about an old man pretending to sulk. The only cute thing at the Saveur was my friend Tomo, who used to work here part-time. Unfortunately, she'd finished grad school and gotten a job, so she was no longer at the coffee shop. From what I heard, however, she and Takano were keeping up their "friendship."

Sabu was still complaining as the owner gently placed my coffee in front of me.

"Last night, Sabu wandered in, and I let it slip," the owner said, sounding apologetic. His eyes, on the other hand, showed he was curious to know more.

"The two of you both knew Momoko before, right?"

"Naturally. How many years do you think I've been hanging around this neighborhood?" Sabu said, sounding quite proud of himself.

"Mr. Morisaki was married before? It doesn't fit my image of him." At some point, Takano had come out of the kitchen carrying plates and towels in both hands, and he eagerly joined the conversation.

"That's right," Sabu said. "You never knew. He's really sort of a widower, isn't he? But when he was young, those two used to make out in front of everyone. It was quite a show, wasn't it?"

"There was a bit of that, I guess," the owner said. "At any rate, Momoko is still beautiful, isn't she? When she came in, she said, 'It makes me so happy to have your coffee after all this time.' She looked like she was doing really well."

"Oh, you're a soft touch. She just wanted to flatter you. If you ask me, she suddenly comes home after being missing for years, she'd better have more than a few jokes. Satoru should run her off straight away. If my wife tried that, I'd knock her down." As he talked, Sabu worked himself up to such a state of excitement that his face turned all red like an octopus.

"Hold on now, Sabu. You sound so aggressive. But whenever your wife tries to make you get rid of some books, aren't you the one begging her in tears?"

When we heard that, Takano and I both burst out laughing.

"Hey, shut up! What are you laughing about, Takano? Get back to work!"

"Sorry, sorry." Takano fled to the back in a hurry as Sabu threw a towel at him.

"If you're ticked off, don't take it out on my staff," the owner said with an exasperated look on his face.

"Aren't you the one who normally bullies him?"

"That I do out of love. Love," the owner said earnestly, "whereas the feeling your wife inspires in you is . . . fear."

"You've always been a real jerk, haven't you? Fine. I'm angry. I'm pissed. Okay. How about I have some stern words with Momoko for Satoru. We know that nincompoop will never be able to say anything."

"Hey now, stop butting into other people's business."

The owner was chiding Sabu, even though he was the one who got Sabu riled up in the first place.

Wow. This neighborhood definitely attracts its share of weirdos.

The thought made me smile, but then Sabu took aim at me. "Takako, quit smirking there by yourself. It's unpleasant."

Right after this, there was another little development at the Saveur. Around nine, Sabu stopped making a fuss and went home (probably because if he didn't get back early his wife would've let him have it), so I moved to sit at a table. As the night wore on, there were only a few customers left. I ordered another coffee, and promptly took the book I'd been reading from my bag and opened it up to my page. Then I noticed something. There was someone I recognized sitting by the window.

He was a slim man in his late twenties. He wore a pale blue shirt with gray pants. His hair was cut short and neatly trimmed. There was nothing flashy about him, but there was something appealing about how neat he was. He was staring out the window absentmindedly, with a half-read paperback lying facedown on the table. He looked as if he were waiting for someone.

Who was he? As I stared at him, thinking this over, he suddenly turned to me as if he'd noticed I was looking at him.

When our eyes met, we both looked surprised. He looked at me and then at the paperback I was holding, then again back and forth, as if he were comparing the two, then he nodded as if he'd understood, and quietly said, "Hello."

Hearing his voice, I finally remembered where I'd met him before. How could I have forgotten? He was someone I'd dealt with many times at the Morisaki Bookshop. Because we were inundated with extremely idiosyncratic regulars—with Sabu chief among them—it was harder for someone a bit more withdrawn like him to make a strong impression. So it just took me a moment to remember him. I was flustered as I returned his greeting, embarrassed about having stared at him so shamelessly.

"Nice to see you. It's been a while," I said, and quickly bowed, but he smiled and said, "Oh, there's no need to be so formal." He had a nice smile that put you at ease.

Right at that moment, the waitress arrived at my table, carrying my coffee on her tray. She was standing directly between the two of us and seemed confused about what to do in the situation. I got caught up in it too and started feeling flustered.

Seeing this, he shyly offered an invitation. "Would you like to sit here?"

"Would you by any chance be waiting for someone?" I asked hesitantly.

"Not especially at the moment," he replied.

Hearing this, the waitress regained her confidence and her smile. "In that case, here it is," she said, quickly placing my coffee in front of his seat.

To which I responded, "I guess I'll sit here then," as I moved to the seat across from him.

In times like this, I tend to get sort of carried away. *He had just been kind enough to invite me over. It wasn't that he especially wanted to talk to me. Now I was interrupting his alone time.* Once I started thinking this way, I felt I needed to apologize.

When I reached my new seat, the waitress told us to take our time, then she bowed and left us. We watched her walk away before we turned to face each other again.

Silence.

Well, this is awkward, I thought as I shifted in my seat. Then he started to laugh to himself quietly. I stared at him blankly.

"Sorry," he said, "this sort of feels like a setup for an arranged marriage."

The smile on his face won me over and I burst out laughing.

"We haven't properly introduced ourselves," he said, clearing his throat. "My name is Akira—Akira Wada." He said he worked at a publishing company nearby that mostly dealt in textbooks and teaching materials.

When I introduced myself, he said, "That's right, Takako! I remember the cheerful owner of the shop was always yelling out 'Takako! Takako!' in a loud voice." He nodded again and again as he laughed.

My face turned red. "Ah, that would be my uncle," I murmured.

"Really, your uncle? It must be great to have a relative who runs a used bookshop," Wada exclaimed, sounding genuinely jealous. "But you're no longer working at the shop?"

"Yeah, for one reason or another, I ended up staying there for a while and working at the shop in exchange for room and board. I guess you could say I was there long enough to recharge my batteries."

"Recharge your batteries? At the shop?"

"Yes."

"I like that, recharge your batteries," Wada exclaimed again. "But to get to do it at a used bookshop, now that sounds luxurious. Oh man, I'm jealous." Then he went on what was almost a little monologue about how if it had been him, he would've never left, he would've just kept on recharging his batteries forever.

Somehow the idea of living at a used bookshop seemed to ignite something within him. He was turning out to be a surprisingly humorous guy.

"Oh, how's your girlfriend doing?" I asked. "I used to see you together a lot." He was still oohing and aahing about living in a bookstore when I remembered her.

Wada used to come to the shop by himself for the most part, but occasionally he brought a girl with him. She was slim and tall like him, and the two of them looked good together. But she didn't seem especially interested in books. Wada would be carefully examining the books with this earnest expression on his face while she was off on her own looking bored. When she finally got tired of waiting for him, she'd get miffed and say, "Still not done yet?" and he would desperately apologize, "Sorry, just a little longer!" Sabu used to say, "Going to a used bookshop as a couple is a preposterous idea," but watching the back-and-forth between them gave you a sense of how close they were. I thought it was charming.

"Oh, I remember those days." The tone of his voice dropped in response to my question. "I'm afraid I've been dumped," he added and laughed dryly. Then he got a rather distant look in his eye.

"I'm sorry!" I apologized right away. I was ready to throw myself at his feet.

"No, no, I don't mind at all," Wada said, trying not to make a big deal of it, but still with that distant look in his eye.

So in our first talk, I'd gone and stepped on a landmine. I was in a colossal panic. I was searching desperately for a new topic to talk about when my gaze stopped at the book lying on the table.

"What is it you're reading there?"

"Ah, it's a book called *Up the Hill*. Actually, I think I got it from the hundred-yen section at Morisaki Bookshop."

Wada picked up the book and showed it to me. I secretly breathed a sigh of relief that we'd moved on from the last topic.

"Oh? I don't know it. Is it a good book?"

"It's hard to say, actually. It's kind of one of those tragic love stories. The author is a guy who had this one book and ended up dying in obscurity. When you read it, the writing can be clumsy, and there are a lot of places where it feels like it's missing something. But there's something about it that fascinates me. I've read it around five times already."

As he talked, he was staring at the oil painting of a road in the hills on the book jacket. There was something tender in the loving way he looked at the book that ended up making me want to read it.

"Really? Five times? Maybe I should check it out."

"I'm not sure I can really recommend it. What are you reading, Takako?"

When I took the book out of my bag, he said, "Oh, Taruho Inagaki? He's great." He looked at me with a glint in his eye.

I guess I should've known from how often he came to the store that he knew much more about books than I did.

"Even though I worked at a bookshop, I don't know all that much about books. I feel like I've barely scratched the surface."

"I don't think it really matters whether you know a lot about books or not. That said, I don't know that much myself. But I think what matters far more with a book is how it affects you."

"You think so? My uncle always says something like that."

"You were always behind the counter in the back, lost in your book. It used to make me curious about what on earth you could be reading."

"Really? I'm so sorry. I was a terrible employee."

"No, that's not what I meant," Wada said, and he looked at me like he was trying to remember something. "You just fit in so well in the store that I wanted to let you be. It was almost like that moment when you're watching a butterfly coming out of its chrysalis, and you're holding your breath, and you want to keep on watching . . . I guess you left a big impression on me. That's why when I saw you there a second ago with a book in your hand, I remembered you right away. I said, 'It's the woman from that bookshop.'"

The thought of being seen like that by someone I didn't know left me feeling terribly embarrassed. But, in those days, I really was like a butterfly waiting patiently to come out of its chrysalis. As I turned page after page, I was waiting for my chance to take flight. So it might not be out of the question that Wada could sense that when he looked at me. I'm not entirely sure though that I've learned to fly that well.

"If I'd never gone to the shop, I'd still be living my life in a daze. I met so many people there, and I learned so many things, and, of course, there were all of the books I discovered. I feel like I finally learned to see something a tiny bit valuable within myself. That's why I know that I'll never forget the days I spent at the book-shop." Although this was the first time I'd ever really spoken to him, the words came pouring out of my mouth with such force I couldn't help myself.

Wada nodded along as he listened with a look of admiration on his face. "To think that all that drama was going on while I knew nothing about it. Man, oh man." He might have been seri-ous, but his way of putting it was oddly funny.

It was also strange—it felt like we'd been friends forever, like I could talk to him for hours. When Wada seemed like he was listening to me seriously, he'd come out with something funny and make me laugh.

That's how we ended up talking for such a long time. When I happened to glance at the clock on the wall, it was already almost eleven o'clock. "Oh, they'll be closing soon," I said, surprised.

"What?" Wada looked caught off guard as well.

His home was nearby, so Wada was going to stay till they closed. I decided to leave a little ahead of him.

"I'm here most nights. We should talk again sometime," he said, smiling as we said goodbye.

After I'd finished paying at the register near the entrance,

I noticed the owner was furtively glancing at me from behind the counter. I had a pretty good idea what he was thinking, so I glared at him, until he made a show of muttering aloud, "I'm busy, busy, busy," and retreating to the back.

Once I'd gone outside, I could see Wada through the window of the Saveur, sitting there with his chin resting in his hand, staring out. I bowed to him, thinking he might be looking at me, but he didn't seem to notice. I turned and started walking to the station. My body felt strangely light, like my feet were floating above the ground.

How weird, I muttered to myself.

When I looked up, I saw the nearly full moon, missing just a sliver on the left, floating in the night sky.

5

"Let's go on a trip together, just the two of us."

When Momoko sprung this question on me, it was about two weeks after I'd seen her for the first time in years.

"There's a really great spot in Okutama," she said, with a glint in her eye.

I nodded, feeling a bit cornered.

"There's a huge mountain, and on the peak is a historic shrine. The scenery is wonderful, and the air is so pure. It's amazing. There's a lovely inn on the mountain, where we can stay and take it easy for a bit. A girls' trip. What do you think?"

When I tried to imagine just the two of us going on a trip together, I started to feel a little uneasy. But she was holding my hands in hers, squeezing them tight, and I could see in her eyes that she was waiting for me to say yes. I had the overwhelming feeling that I was being pressured into it.

In the two weeks between our reunion and this invitation, I'd been visiting the bookshop fairly often. Of course, I was there to spy on Momoko for my uncle. He and I often crossed paths as he was leaving work, but Momoko was always in the room on the second floor.

Whenever I visited, Momoko was very happy to see me. And she always treated me to a home-cooked meal. When I lived there, the kitchen on the second floor had felt too small, so I never felt much like cooking there, but Momoko made all kinds of things.

She simmered hijiki seaweed, beef with tofu, octopus and daikon. She fried horse mackerel nanbanzuke-style, grilled pike mackerel in salt, made miso soup with daikon greens, radishes, and fried tofu. I was so starved for the taste of home cooking that I basically started coming just for the food. When I called her at lunch from the office, Momoko would act like a new bride, always asking, "What do you feel like eating today?" To which I'd respond by blithely requesting whatever I was in the mood for.

At first, Momoko kept saying it was her treat, so I didn't ask, but after a while, I insisted on splitting the cost and paying for half the groceries.

"Okey dokey," she said, happy to oblige.

"Momoko, everything you make is delicious," I said, and I meant it. I was eating my way through some of the dishes she had spread out on the little dining table as usual.

"Well, you always eat with such enthusiasm. You make it look delicious," Momoko said as she proceeded to devour twice as much as what I ate. I could never figure out how she managed to fit so much food in her tiny frame.

"But it really is delicious," I said, crunching on a pickled radish. "Don't you cook?"

"I cook a little, but just things like pasta. Never anything like this."

"Well, then what'll you do when you have a boyfriend?"

"You think it'll be a problem?"

It's true that I didn't have much experience regaling my boyfriends with my cooking. The idea of cooking for someone made me so embarrassed that I'd avoided it up to this point. Anyway, it's not like I had much experience with relationships in the first place.

"Men are simple. It doesn't matter who they are. You can always seduce them with food." She laughed and said, "I'll teach you. You just try to remember." I wasn't sure I had a sense of how men felt. In fact, it seemed more like the person Momoko was winning over was me.

Of course, I didn't forget my uncle's request entirely. I tried to get her to talk. But Momoko always managed to evade my questions. When I asked her something in earnest, she'd just say, "Oh, I don't know." No matter how I tried to pin her down, she'd wriggle away like an eel. She was already someone who seemed to jump from one topic to another without rhyme or reason, so she'd always end up going off on a tangent. And once the food was spread out in front of me, I would fall into a trance and completely forget to ask about anything else. That's basically how it went every time, so I didn't really make much progress.

Nevertheless, I was able to learn a few things about her. (When Momoko got drunk, she tended to let her guard down and tell me more, so I often urged her to keep drinking.) She lost her parents early on and was raised by her aunt and uncle in Niigata. After middle school, she worked at a small factory, then left for Tokyo on her own at twenty-one, where, among other things, she fell in love with an up-and-coming photographer ("Is that for real?" I couldn't help asking).

Momoko lived for a time in Paris because her boyfriend had gone over for work, and she chased after him. She decided on her own to go without talking with her boyfriend. A bold move, but very Momoko.

"I was young, you know. I was just a girl who didn't know anything, and he was all I thought of. Later I found out that he had a wife and kids back in Japan. That's why it ended. The idea that to have the family I'd always wanted I'd have to destroy someone else's . . . It was just too much." Momoko stared off into the distance as she told me the story.

She couldn't see any future in their relationship, and, in the end, it all fell apart. She was brokenhearted. That's when she happened to meet my uncle Satoru. At first, she saw him as someone who needed looking after. She helped him take care of a few things, and before she knew it, they'd fallen in love.

"I never knew about any of that," I said, impressed by how much history they shared.

"My past makes Satoru jealous. So he doesn't like to talk about it much," Momoko said with a shrug.

Meanwhile, Momoko sussed out the real reason for my frequent visits. It happened one night once it had become perfectly routine for us to eat together. In between sips of sake, Momoko grinned to herself and suddenly said, "Satoru asked you to do this, right, Takako?"

"Huh? What do you mean?" I said, privately panicking as I attempted to keep up the charade. But it was no use. Momoko looked exceptionally happy as she reached over and pinched my cheek.

"I understand what he's thinking. But Takako, deep down, do I make you uncomfortable?"

My heart was racing as she pinched my cheek as hard as she liked. Somehow she had seen through the whole thing. It was true that there was a little part of me that didn't really love being with her. I definitely didn't dislike her, but if someone asked, I'd have been hard-pressed to say that I loved her. That's how it felt. If someone asked about her cooking, on the other hand, I would've answered right away that I loved it.

To be honest, I found her a tough person to figure out. My uncle was similar in that sense. There was something I couldn't grasp about him, but she was different. It felt like no matter how many times I talked to her, I could never close the gap between us. Sometimes it felt like we were standing on opposite sides of a river, talking to one another from across an enormous divide.

"It's okay, because I love you, Takako. And I think it's cute how honest you are. You can't tell a lie. It makes me wish I had a beautiful soul like that."

"I definitely do not have a beautiful soul."

I felt like she might be making fun of me, and I was a little offended.

But Momoko said she really meant it. "I just lie all the time," she said, sounding lonely somehow. For a moment, she hung her head.

Her facial expression revealed something in that instant that was not lost on me. I felt like it was the first time I had gotten close to what Momoko was really feeling.

But it only lasted an instant.

Immediately afterward, her face lit up, and she became her normal self again and changed the subject. Which is when she proposed her idea: "Hey, how about going on a trip together? It's too early for the fall foliage, but that means that there won't be many people and we can take our time. Are you busy at work?" She kept going on and on like this as she put pressure on me.

"No, it's a relatively flexible company."

"So, we're good?"

"Um, well . . ."

At first, I thought I would try to say no, but for some reason the expression I'd seen on her face had left me worried. So in the end, I agreed. "Let's do it."

I can't quite explain why, but I sensed something then. It wasn't exactly a premonition—nothing as grandiose as that. It was something I couldn't put into words, but I definitely felt it when I saw her face, like it was a sign I shouldn't ignore.

I saw Wada two more times at the Saveur before our conversation about the trip. Both times, I was stopping by the coffee shop on my way home from seeing Momoko, and he was there. He'd said he came often, and it seemed to be true. He was sitting at the same seat by the window when I saw him, staring out the window as he had before.

I wasn't entirely sure myself whether or not I went there because I wanted to see Wada. I don't think I went to the coffee shop expecting anything in particular. But when I walked in and I caught sight of Wada from behind, I heard myself say, "Oh."

I said hello, and his shoulders trembled like I'd woken him up from a dream. He stared at me for about five seconds as if he were verifying something about me, then he smiled and said hello.

He seemed to be asking me to join him, so I took a seat across from him and we talked. It was just small talk, nothing special, but just talking together made me feel strangely at ease. One time we even left together before the coffee shop closed and went on a little walk to the Imperial Palace.

"See you soon."

"Bye."

That's how we said goodbye, even though we didn't have each other's contact info, and there was no guarantee that we'd ever meet again.

After that night, I went to the coffee shop a third time, but Wada wasn't there. I knew there was no reason for me to expect him to be around, but I still somehow felt let down. I felt like I'd come for no reason. But I persuaded myself that it would actually be weirder if he were there all the time.

That night, I took a seat at the counter and tried subtly asking the owner about Wada.

He'd seen me talking to him, so of course he remembered him.

"He's a bit of a quiet customer. These days, as soon as it gets dark, he comes in. But I don't remember if he used to come before too."

"He isn't quiet. He's reserved." I said, gently correcting the owner.

"Oh, forgive me. He does seem like the type who tends to stay a while."

Then Takano joined in from across the room to offer an absurd suggestion. "Isn't he coming to see Takako? From back here, they do kind of look good together."

I stared at him with my mouth hanging wide open for a second, and then I furiously denied everything. "That's ridiculous!"

"Aw, come on, don't be mad."

"You'd better stop butting in!" the owner said, running him off.

Takano yelled, "Sorry!" as he fled the room.

As I lifted the coffee cup to my lips, I thought about what Takano had said one more time. *That can't be, can it?* And I told myself again that Takano had to be wrong.

But . . . but what if it was true?

Wada was a great guy. He was friendly and polite, and he had a good sense of humor. And he knew a lot about books, of course, too. He wasn't always boasting about himself or laughing crudely at his own jokes. With his personality, I'm sure lots of women were attracted to him.

Well, what about me?

Just as I was contemplating the question, I realized the owner was staring at me again.

"You should work on your habit of watching people so intensely. Especially when it comes to girls. They'll resent you," I said coldly.

The owner laughed his high-pitched laugh as he hurried after Takano and disappeared into the back of the coffee shop.

I had lost my urge to think through the question, so instead I took out the book Wada had told me about, *Up the Hill*, and gave it a try. When I was visiting Momoko earlier, I'd come across it by chance on one of the shelves at the bookshop around closing time.

When he saw the book in my hand, my uncle took it upon himself to tell me, "It's nothing special."

"I don't mind," I said. I handed my uncle one hundred yen and bought the book.

It's a short novel, about two hundred pages long. That night, first at the Saveur and then back at home before bed, I read the whole thing.

It was a sad story, just as Wada had said.

The story is set in Tokyo, during the period when the country was rebuilding after the war. The main character is an unsuccessful writer named Matsugorō Ida. He meets a beautiful woman who works at a "modern" café up the hill. For him, it's love at first sight. At first, she doesn't take him seriously, but Matsugorō keeps going to the café every day, and, after he confesses his love to her, he and the cheerful Ukiyō become a couple. But just when you think the happy days might last forever, Ukiyō is forced to marry the son of a wealthy man to pay off her father's debts. With barely any prospects for his own future, Matsugorō has no way to stop the wedding.

Matsugorō keeps on writing novels through his loneliness and despair. His sole motivation is the idea that if he becomes famous and makes a name for himself in the world, he might be able to get Ukiyō back. Finally, when he's in his late thirties, Matsugorō's dream comes true, and he finds success as a novelist. But that's when he discovers the awful truth: Ukiyō has succumbed to an epidemic and is no longer in this world.

From that time on, Matsugorō spends his days drowning himself in alcohol, women, and then drugs. His dissipated life leaves his body battered. But he never lets himself forget Ukiyō, not even for a moment, and he keeps going to the café where they first met every day. Then, one day, on his way home from the café, he collapses, coughing up blood. As he loses consciousness, all that remains in his heart is his memory of Ukiyō.

Matsugorō's painful, single-minded obsession hit home for me. After I finished the book, my heart fell silent. Tears ran down my cheeks and dropped onto the book, leaving little stains on the pages.

Under the covers of my futon, as I drifted off to sleep, I found myself thinking that Wada had a pretty romantic side.

In my dream that night, I was the woman who ran the café in the novel, and I was shaking Ukiyō by the shoulders, doing my best to persuade her to go out with Matsugorō.

6

"Why do you have to go on a trip with her?"

The night before we were to leave, I got a call from my uncle. I was working at the office, the last person still there. He said he'd just heard from Momoko about the trip. "I asked you to find out what was going on with her," he said, sounding disconcerted, "but you didn't have to go this far."

"It just sort of happened as we were talking," I responded vaguely. I wasn't feeling able at that particular moment to explain exactly how it happened.

"Knowing her, I bet she just forced you to go along with her," my uncle said, sounding worried.

"No, it wasn't like that."

"I don't know," my uncle said, still worrying.

"I'll bring you home a present," I said cheerfully.

"If you're okay with it, Takako, that's good enough for me, I guess," he said, reluctantly conceding. "By the way, Sabu keeps storming into the shop and saying he wants to see Momoko. What the hell's going on?"

I remembered the little drama at the Saveur and laughed out loud.

"He seems to want to have a word with her."

"What?" I could hear my uncle's astonishment on the other end of the phone. "Momoko will roll right over him, and then she'll flatter him and he'll end up going home happy. She's weirdly good at dealing with guys like him."

I could see the whole scene vividly in my mind.

"I think you're right."

"No doubt about it. But Momoko mostly goes out around lunchtime, so she isn't here when Sabu comes, which makes him angry."

"Is that right?"

"And even if I subtly try to ask her where she's going, she won't tell me."

It was my turn to be astonished. "Because she's not a child," I said. "As long as she comes back afterward, does it really matter?"

"I guess that's true ... Anyway, you don't have to go on this trip if you don't want to. I don't know why she asked you ..." he went on muttering and then he finally hung up.

That night, after finishing work, I decided to drop by the Saveur again. By the time I left the office, it was already after nine, and I didn't feel like going home, so I ended up there. The place was still crowded. Wada's usual spot by the window was occupied by two girls.

I found a seat at a table and read slowly from the book I bought for my trip—*Friendship* by Saneatsu Mushanokōji—but I couldn't really concentrate. Although I didn't mean to, every time someone came into the coffee shop, I'd find myself looking toward the door, thinking it might be Wada.

I had only managed to make it through about twenty pages when Wada showed up for real. I greeted him with a slight bow, feeling flustered, and he came slowly over to where I was sitting. Seeing him from that distance, I got a strange feeling. He seemed less lively than usual.

I waited until he had taken a seat before I asked any questions. "Have you been busy at work?"

"No, on the contrary, things have been slow." Wada smiled as he said it, but his face showed how tired he was.

We both fell silent for a moment. Normally, I wouldn't worry about a moment of silence between us, but for some reason, I felt a heaviness in the air. I thought of what Takano had said, and then it got even harder to make conversation.

"That reminds me . . ." I said with a smile, remembering something good to tell him. "I read *Up the Hill*."

But Wada didn't seem to take much of an interest. "Oh, is that right?" he mumbled. I'd selfishly expected he would be happy to hear this. I felt dejected that my expectations were so far off the mark.

"The story is a bit of a cliché, don't you think?" Wada said with a touch of irony.

"No way. I loved the book."

"But the whole idea of waiting for someone you love till the day you die. That kind of thing never happens in the real world."

"Is that right?"

"At least that's what I think. Instead, the person you love just comes out and tells you you're being creepy."

"Huh?" I had no idea what he was talking about. But Wada went on speaking in fits and starts.

"When she and I first met, I brought her here. She liked the place, so after that day, she and I came here a lot. That's why I told her I'm still waiting for her here. 'If you change your mind,' I said, 'come look for me here.' Well, the day before yesterday, she sends me an email making herself perfectly clear: 'You're being creepy. Stop.'"

At this point, I'd heard enough to understand what he'd meant earlier. *So that's what's been going on. If only he'd told me sooner. No, but why would he tell me?*

He'd been waiting all this time—waiting for the beautiful woman he used to bring to the bookshop. He was just like Matsugorō waiting for Ukiyō. Or rather, was that why he transferred all those emotions to the novel and kept reading it over and over?

Oh, what the hell. I kept repeating the words to myself again and again. It's not that I was particularly sad. Somehow deep down I'd always had the feeling that he didn't think of me like that. I just felt like a complete idiot for letting myself get so worked up over everything.

What about the weird way we could talk and talk? Or the way we felt like old friends? None of that was real. Wada was kind enough to listen to me, and I took advantage of that and talked about myself. That's what really made me feel good. I felt so guilty when I finally realized this.

"I'm sorry. It's not a very interesting story," Wada said apologetically, perhaps because he'd noticed that I'd been looking down all this time.

I shook my head. "No, I'm the one who should apologize."

"What? Why should you apologize, Takako?" Wada seemed surprised.

"Just because."

"Huh?"

I really wanted to apologize more, but I also didn't want him to think I was weird, so I held back. I've got to change the subject, I thought, but I also felt the urge to ask more bubbling up inside me.

"You loved her, didn't you?" I blurted out, and then immediately regretted it.

Wada smiled a little.

"I hate to admit how childish the whole thing was. But, you know, I can understand it too. At first, she and I didn't seem to have anything in common. There was no way for things to work out between us. But it's like I was stubborn about it. I fell in love with her. And for some reason I could never just see that we were too different and we'd be better off ending things. I've always thought of myself as a rather sober person, but I discovered I have a passionate side. It came as a bit of a surprise."

He could've skipped the analysis at this point. I guess he was a little weird after all.

"I think you're a good person," I said, trying to cheer him up. I wish I could've come up with something better to say, but nothing else came to mind. I meant it sincerely though. Wada was a really good person.

"Thank you. If you say so, I must be a decent human being. That much is true," he said, laughing softly. "But I got told, 'You're a good person, but you're not interesting.'"

"Don't you think she was being a bit cruel?" I said. I was getting a little angry at this woman. I felt like she couldn't recognize the goodness in him.

"No," Wada said. "Because I agree with her. So much so that I was actually impressed by how well she'd hit the nail on the head. But this is a boring subject, let's drop it." Wada tried to change the subject and get me to open up by asking how I'd been recently. But I was still feeling hurt, and I couldn't contribute to the conversation.

"Sorry, I've got an early start tomorrow . . ." The conversation never seemed to get any more cheerful. I kept it going a little longer and then I excused myself and got up.

"Oh really?" Wada looked at me a little blankly.

When I tried to leave, the owner called out from near the door. "Are you going home, Takako?"

"Yes" was all I said before I walked out.

I was in a dark mood. The owner must've realized it too. I didn't feel much like coming back for a while.

As I walked, I felt more and more depressed. I must've sighed about thirty times. By the time I realized that I'd forgotten my book on the table, I was already on the train home.

7

I met up with Momoko at Shinjuku Station at ten.

It was cloudy, but according to the weather forecast on TV, the sky was going to clear up in the afternoon.

I was using up my vacation days to go on this trip, so before I left home, I tried to give myself a pep talk: *Don't let last night drag you down.*

Momoko showed up at the jam-packed south entrance of Shinjuku Station, carrying so little—just a backpack that could've been mistaken for a child's—you would've never guessed she was leaving on a trip. Her hair was tied back in a bun, and she wore a green hoodie and black tracksuit pants. She was so small that from a distance, she looked like a schoolgirl on a field trip.

When Momoko saw my outfit, she furrowed her brow. "Oh my," she said, "you're not dressed like someone who's going to the mountains, are you?" This was my first trip in a long time, and I was decked out in a dress I'd just bought on sale.

"I did put on sneakers though," I said, trying to explain myself. "And I have some proper hiking clothes in my bag."

"You didn't need to pack so much," Momoko said.

That shut me up. I was embarrassed by how much I'd been looking forward to the trip. Perhaps to make up for what she'd said, Momoko added, "I guess that's just what it's like being young. You're always carrying around a lot of luggage."

"And when you're old, you have less?" I countered.

"It's fine for you, Takako. I just don't like anything weighing me down," she said dryly.

"That makes sense," I said, convinced.

"Anyway, thank you for coming. Here's to a good three-day trip," Momoko said. She straightened her posture and bowed theatrically.

"I should be the one thanking you," I said, bowing.

We took the Chūō line from Shinjuku, and changed to the Ōme line at Tachikawa Station. In the roughly five years since I'd moved to Tokyo, this was my first time heading that way. The train cars on the Ōme line were fairly empty. Sitting in the seats across from us was a high school student, a bit of a bad boy type, who looked like he'd overslept. He sat there with a sullen expression on his face, restlessly tapping his foot. He looked angry at the whole world.

Momoko took her seat and stared out the window, humming to herself. The night before I'd been up till dawn, thinking of one thing or another, none of it very interesting. Once I settled in on the train, I was asleep before I knew it.

When I woke up a little while later, the bad boy high schooler was long gone. He'd probably gone to school angry.

I glanced out the window, and I saw that at some point the clouds had disappeared and blue sky now stretched into the distance. There were far fewer houses and buildings, and the mountains in the distance beyond the farmland and rice paddies were growing bigger and bigger.

"Amazing," I said, rubbing my eyes.

"Just wait till you see what's next," Momoko said with a grin.

We got off the train at a little station called Mitake. The mountains were right in front of us now, with the blue sky behind them, and in the center of it all was an enormous mountain that towered over everything else. It was a majestic, massive mountain—it was not going to budge one bit. The leaves hadn't really started to change color yet for fall, so the mountain was still a deep green. Somewhere up there was the inn we were heading to.

"We're not far from the center of the city, but it feels like we've gone a really long way," I muttered, looking at the scenery in front of me. I took a deep breath and filled my lungs with fresh, clean air. It was impressive to see how much nature was still left within the city limits.

"It only took a few decades for the city to fill up with all those buildings," Momoko said.

It made me think of the short story "Musashino" in one of Doppo Kunikida's books. At the beginning of the twentieth century, when Doppo was alive, the area around Musashino was still so wild you could lose yourself inside it. These days it's just another neighborhood in Tokyo. The times change so quickly. It was enough to leave you dizzy.

At the little stop in front of the station, we caught a bus that took us on the highway to the starting point of the funicular, halfway up the mountain. By the time we got to the bus stop, two tour groups that had probably arrived on the same train as us had already taken their seats. Both were groups of elderly men and women. It was a mystery though what had brought them all here together. We gave a quick bow and sat down next to them. The oldest-looking woman in the group smiled and said, "On a little mother-daughter trip?"

"Yes," Momoko said, smiling back.

We're not mother and daughter, I thought, but it was too

much trouble to explain our relationship, so I nodded and let the expression on my face say, *That's my mom, and I'm her daughter.*

As soon as we got on the bus, three grade-school-age boys started talking to us. They were apparently quite used to tourists because they didn't seem the slightest bit shy. Momoko seemed to like kids. She gave them a big smile and started happily chatting with them. "What grade are you guys in?" she asked.

"First!" they answered in unison, full of enthusiasm.

They told us their families ran inns up on the mountain, so they had to come down the mountain every day to go to school.

"That must be hard," I said, which was probably what tourists always said to them.

"I suppose," one replied, sounding quite grown-up. It was like he was saying, "Oh, *now* you tell me."

"Come on, come on!" they shouted. Letting the kids lead us, we got off the bus and climbed the mountain road to the funicular station. The kids were running fast, and I quickly ended up a little out of breath as I brought up the rear. Momoko turned around and looked at me.

"Takako, you know the real climbing doesn't start until after the funicular. If you're already tired, I don't know what we're going to do with you," she teased.

The kids burst out laughing. "Lady, you're never going to make it. This is what happens when you grow up in the city," one said, and they laughed again.

"Actually, I grew up way out in the country in Kyushu," I said, trying to argue the point from the back, but they were going so quickly and I had fallen so far behind that no one seemed to hear me. Why was Momoko in such great shape? The age difference between us was enough for people to mistake us for mother and daughter. I was starting to regret that I hadn't packed lighter.

When I finally made it to the base of the funicular, Momoko handed me a bottle of tea she'd bought at a gift shop. "Here you go," she said.

I accepted gratefully and gulped it all down.

The funicular took us up the mountain like the tracks were running along a stream. It dropped us off just before the summit. Then we waved goodbye to the kids and began to trudge uphill again. We'd already made it to nearly one thousand meters above sea level. It was hard to believe that just an hour ago we'd been at the foot of the mountain.

Along the narrow road that led to the peak were signs with advertisements and directions for each inn. "Our inn is the farthest, so it's going to take forty minutes," Momoko said casually.

"What?" I whined.

"But the view is incredible," she said, and pinched my cheek.

More stairs and steep slopes followed. There was only one little store and a single rest stop. Everything else was either a mountain inn or a private residence. Each time someone coming down from the peak passed us, they greeted us with a cheerful "Hello!"

And each time, Momoko and I answered back enthusiastically, "Hello!"

The overwhelming majority of the people we saw were elderly, but there were some young couples and large groups of what looked like college students. I felt a tiny bit relieved to see that most of the young people were dressed in normal clothes like I was.

Finally, the inn we'd been looking for came into view. At this point, I was completely out of breath. Momoko seemed to be feeling the strain a bit too. "We made it. We made it," she said, sighing as she wiped the sweat from her forehead with a towel.

The wooden building looked pretty worn down. It had three floors that seemed to be joined to a private home. The back of the building was right up against the cliff. In the large yard out front, someone had left out a tractor, a rusty bicycle, and some logs. The place had a very lived-in look. To put it nicely, I guess you could call it unpretentious. To put it not so nicely, it was a dump. But I had trouble imagining Momoko staying at some neat little inn. So I took one look and thought, This looks great.

"Is anyone there?" Momoko opened the door and yelled inside. After a moment, we heard the sound of someone running down the hall, and a young girl appeared.

She was dressed in loose jeans and a sweatshirt that was clearly too big for her. She looked about twenty years old.

The girl looked at Momoko and spoke so bluntly you never would've guessed she was talking to a guest. "Hey, is that Momoko?"

"It's been a while, Haru. How've you been?" Momoko replied.

"Who's this? She your daughter? Wait, you have children?"

"I'm her niece, Takako," I said, introducing myself to Haru before Momoko could tell another person I was her daughter.

Haru might be a little bit rough around the edges, but she didn't seem particularly mean-spirited.

"Nice to meet you," she said, and gave a quick bow in my direction.

We heard footsteps from inside again. This time a woman in her fifties came slowly walking toward us, dressed in an apron coverall and a headscarf.

"Ah, Momoko, you're early," the woman said with a friendly smile. She had a brisk way of talking, but you could sense that she was someone who liked taking care of people.

"It's nice to see you again," Momoko said, and bowed properly. I realized the woman in the apron was the innkeeper.

"Hey, Momoko," Haru said, "you gonna work here again?"

"No, Haru. Momoko came as a guest today."

"Oh no, really?"

Seeing me marvel at this back-and-forth, Momoko whispered in my ear. "When I left Satoru's, I moved up here for a little while and the innkeeper gave me a job."

"So that's what happened?" I said, raising my voice in surprise.

"Basically," she replied nonchalantly.

The innkeeper led us to our room. It was only just after 2 p.m., so we were the first guests of the day. The inside of the building was just as messy as the outside. There was stuff everywhere. In the hallway, someone had left an empty aquarium, a huge pile of magazines, an old TV, and an acoustic guitar. When I snuck a peek at the kitchen next to the entryway, it looked pretty chaotic. Same for the toilets, the washroom, and the bath. It felt more like a boardinghouse than an inn. During summer vacation, it was probably filled with students. I don't know whether the other inns on the mountain were similar, but in this inn, the atmosphere was extremely casual.

She led us to a room at the far corner because it had the best view. It was about ten tatami mats large, the perfect size for the two of us.

Outside the window, we were surrounded by dense green foliage. The trees swayed gently in the breeze. Now and then we heard a bird call that might have been a thrush. The mountains in the distance were shrouded in mist. Up above, drifting slowly across the aqua-blue sky, was a group of little, dappled clouds that looked like a school of fish. As I stared at the view, I felt myself losing all sense of time.

I sat by the window for a while, gazing at the scenery. Beside me, Momoko was unusually quiet as she looked at the view, perhaps overcome by the same emotions. I tried to imagine what it must've been like to live and work in a place like this. I surprised myself when I realized I might enjoy it.

Then there was a forceful knocking at the door, and Haru came in. "It's already getting really cold at night," she said, carrying a heavy-looking stove in both hands. She put it down with a thud in a corner of the room.

"Thanks," I said.

"Yup, enjoy!" she replied on her way out, sounding more like a waitress at a bar.

"Momoko, how long did you work here?" I asked.

She cocked her head to one side to think. Then she said, "About three years, I guess."

"What did you do after that?"

"Well, all sorts of stuff. People can live anywhere if they put their mind to it."

That was definitely true in her case. She seemed fierce enough to live anywhere.

"Well," she said, jumping to her feet. "Shall we go out for a bit before dinner?"

We were going to leave the real hiking for the next day, and so we decided to pay our respects to the shrine up the mountain. Momoko said the shrine was just a stone's throw from the inn, and it would take us less than five minutes to get there. When we passed the little corner with its modest gift shop and restaurant, the large torii gate of the shrine appeared before us. We gave a quick bow at the gate and followed a group of people onto the grounds.

The shrine was much nicer than I expected it to be. We passed one sanctuary and treasure hall after another. On the path lead-ing to the main shrine, countless stone monuments crowded side by side. I read a sign that explained its history, and it said the original shrine had been constructed in this location more than 1,200 years ago in the Nara period. From the Middle Ages, the site was considered one of the sacred mountains in the region. Worshippers had flocked to the mountain for centuries.

I was shocked to discover that it had been around for so long. For hundreds of years, so many had made the same trek to visit this shrine. There was no transportation then, so the walk must've taken days or even weeks. It must've meant even more to them than it did to us today. I felt humbled by my lack of faith.

We climbed the steep stone steps to get to the main shrine. There were bright purple blossoms in the wild gentian growing along the route. The stairs seemed to go on forever, and we struggled to make it up to the shrine. The other tourists were breathing hard as they climbed the steps. When we finally stood in front of the hall of worship, I struggled to catch my breath again.

I somehow pulled myself together, and we threw our coins into the collection box and pressed our hands together in prayer.

I looked over at Momoko when I was done, but she was still praying. The expression on her face was extremely serious.

When she opened her eyes again, I asked, "What are you praying for?"

"Nothing."

"But it looked like you were praying with such intensity."

"A shrine isn't where you pray for something. It's a place for you to express gratitude. It's for you to tell the gods, 'Thank you for always watching over me.'"

"Oh, I just asked for something, um, fervently."

"What did you ask for?"

"You know, good health, and that I don't go broke."

Momoko laughed, saying that sounded a lot like me. We did a loop around the grounds of the shrine to look around. Then she said, "When I first left Satoru, I wandered to this shrine. That's how I ended up asking if I could stay at that inn. I didn't have anyone else to turn to, so I asked the innkeeper if I could move in and work there. It turned out that she was actually short-handed at the time. She had just lost her husband, and she didn't have Haru yet. But even so, for her to hire a strange middle-aged woman . . . It was really generous of her."

She likes to talk about herself in the third person, I thought, weirdly impressed.

Before we left, we stood together and bowed again. The main shrine was shining beautifully in the setting sun. Then we went back down the steep path to the inn.

I took a bath to wash away all the sweat. While I was lying around on my futon waiting for Momoko to finish her bath, I was overcome by drowsiness again. When Momoko shook me awake, it was already well past dinnertime.

While I was in dreamland, two other groups of guests had come to the hotel. We all met in the dining hall. One group was composed of three generations of the same family. The other was a pair of middle-aged men. The men were already a little drunk. When we came into the room, they greeted us by shouting, "Sorry, we started without you!" Their voices were ridiculously loud.

There was so much to eat at dinner that it was overwhelming. The innkeeper kept bringing one thing after another. Simmered dishes, fermented soybeans, pickled scallions, kimchi—there were so many different little sides. She even made a hot pot and tempura.

The most delicious dish of all was the ayu sweetfish grilled with miso. After eating that with rice and miso soup, I was full, so I gave my hot pot and tempura to the men. Thanks to the relaxed atmosphere at the inn, there was an unusually festive feeling in the dining hall. The men were both interested in mountain climbing, and they had been to this mountain many times. As blind drunk as they were, they still took the time to tell us all their recommendations for places to visit. I would've liked to have seen the spots where the violets and false anemones grew, but it was too late in the year.

The family said they'd come for a little trip, just to be together as a family before the grandson's wedding. The grandmother was now somewhere between eighty-seven and eighty-nine. (The question of her exact age provoked a brief dispute.) They had to push her wheelchair the whole way from the funicular station to the inn.

"This is my last trip," the grandmother murmured.

"What! You're still so young. You've still got time for lots of trips!" Momoko insisted, looking quite happy.

Later, after the two other groups went upstairs, Momoko launched into a nonstop conversation with the innkeeper, so I went up to the room ahead of her.

When I got back to our room, I thought about what Momoko had been like all day, and came to the conclusion that all my worries about the trip had been in my head. She seemed so happy. She was the same cheerful person she always was. She'd probably just been nostalgic for the place where she used to work.

I'd come all this way with the wrong idea. Just like with

Hideaki. I was someone who took a long time to figure things out. But maybe it didn't matter. I was enjoying myself. That's what I thought as I waited for Momoko.

When Momoko came back to the room, she said, "We've got an early start tomorrow. Let's go to bed," and quickly got under the covers.

But having foolishly taken two naps that day, I couldn't fall asleep.

Momoko was asleep within three minutes of getting into bed. I could hear her breathing peacefully (with the occasional bout of snoring).

As I lay there, I was sorry I'd forgotten my book at the Saveur—not that those regrets did me any good now. Then, at the same moment, Wada's face appeared in my mind.

I wonder what he's doing right now. Probably sleeping. And here I am spending a sleepless night in a strange place. We might not be far from home, but I feel lonely. I really miss him. It wouldn't have killed me to have asked him for his number. Now I might never see him again. He doesn't have any more reason to go to the coffee shop. It hurts to realize that it might be too late now for anything but regret.

The more I thought about it, the more awake I felt, so I quietly snuck out of the room. The whole inn was asleep. But then I saw a light coming from the sliding door of the little room at the end of the hall. Tiptoeing over and sneaking a peek inside, I saw Haru sitting with her legs crossed in front of a desk, scowling at the computer screen. She had the same intense expression on her face that Momoko had when she was praying at the temple.

When I tried to tiptoe away, she noticed me and called out absentmindedly "What's up? Something happen?"

"I just couldn't sleep," I said.

"In that case, maybe you should go for a walk. It's a clear night, the stars should be pretty." She gestured toward the entrance with her chin.

"Maybe I will," I said.

As I was about to walk out the door, I heard, "Wait a sec. It's pitch black out there and it's dangerous for a girl to be all alone." Haru came after me with a flashlight in her hand.

We quietly opened the front door and went into the yard.

Because of the high altitude, we could see our breath even though it was still only the middle of October. When I looked up at the sky, the stars seemed so much closer than usual. There were winter constellations that we wouldn't have seen in the city. Across from the cliffs, they were twinkling over the rolling mountains.

We walked slowly together toward the shrine. Everyone was asleep. There wasn't a single room with a light on. The only noise was the satisfying clip-clop sound of our sandals.

"I'm sorry I dragged you along on this."

"No worries. I was just looking at something online." Haru took a cigarette from her pocket, put it in her mouth, and lit it. Then she stood there looking out at the darkness, exhaling smoke.

"When did you start working here, Haru?"

"Since I graduated high school. The boss is one of my relatives."

"Is that right?"

"Pretty much everybody here's like that. They run the inn with their families and relatives. Beyond that, the local high school kids come to work part-time when they're on break. People like Momoko are pretty unusual."

"Is the job fun?"

"Hard to say. This is the only job I've ever had. It gets pretty busy when the students are here. But this time of year can be a little lonely. Why are you traveling together? You don't seem that close." Haru asked the question without seeming to have any special interest in the answer.

"I don't really know. Before we left, I had the feeling there was something she wanted to tell me, but now it seems like that was just in my head."

"Hmmm . . . Now that you mention it though, back when she was working here, she was in a much darker mood. Seeing her again now, I was kind of surprised to see how cheerful she was."

"Really?"

"Yeah. In her later days here, she was more upbeat, maybe, but when I first started here, she hardly ever talked. She kinda scared me."

I tried to envision Momoko being like that, but I really couldn't do it.

"I don't get it, I guess," she said, and threw her cigarette in the ashtray that had been installed right in front of the torii gate of the shrine.

A shooting star streaked across the night sky and disappeared. At which point, Haru let out a single, massive sneeze.

"Should we head back?" I asked.

Haru sniffled and said, "Sure."

8

The next morning, I couldn't seem to muster the energy to get out from under the covers of my futon. I just lay there dawdling. Momoko tried to rip the covers off me a few times, but I held on tight and fought her tooth and nail.

It was after nine when I finally got up, washed my face, and wandered the inn in search of her.

"She's got to be in the yard," the innkeeper told me, trying to keep from laughing.

When I went outside, I saw Momoko standing in the middle of the yard, drenched in morning light. She was still wearing her yukata from last night, but she was in a funny pose.

"What're you doing?" I asked.

"Tai Chi," she said. She told me it had been a morning routine for years. "It's really good for your health. Plus it makes you feel good. You want to try it with me, sleepyhead?"

Was she doing it every morning at the bookshop? I'm sure the sight of a middle-aged woman doing Tai Chi in front of a second-hand bookstore surprised the businessmen on their way to work. Just imagining it made me almost burst out laughing.

After finishing breakfast, Momoko and I finally left for our hike. Today I was fully prepared, wearing clothes it was much easier to move in. All of the other guests seemed to have started off long before us. When I told Momoko we still had plenty of time, she turned and gave me an icy glare.

As we left the inn, the innkeeper called after us, "See you soon!"

If you went over two mountains on the trail, you'd make it to an overlook with an amazing view. That's where we were headed.

It was nice and cold in the mountains. We were surrounded by cedars, some of them five times my size. When I stopped to have a look at the pretty wildflowers growing here and there along the way, Momoko would point at each and tell me its name. She had only lived here for a few years, but still she knew quite a lot about life here. I, on the other hand, had not been hiking since a summer program in grade school. It was fun to walk in the mountains with such a knowledgeable guide. I didn't have to worry about getting lost. Feeling a little better, I started to hum a song we sang on the weekend trip, "The Bear in the Woods."

But this was only at the very beginning of the hike. After that, I wasn't singing songs anymore. The path, which was flat and wide at first, gradually grew narrower and steeper. It's like it was telling me, "This mountain doesn't mess around." Soon it was hard to find your footing, and I was afraid that if I stopped paying attention for a moment, my feet would slip. One minute, I was blithely singing, "And this is what the bear said!" The next, I felt like I was trapped in a bottomless pit, too uncoordinated to find my way out.

But Momoko didn't seem to think the path was bad at all. She kept going, nimbly making her way, showing no mercy. When the distance between us grew too wide, she would stop and wait for me to catch up.

"Hey, um, Miss Mountain Guide, can we slow down a bit?" I grumbled, around the time we had just passed the gigantic boulder known as Tengu Rock, because it looked a little like that mythical creature with the long nose.

"I wonder whose fault it is that we don't have much time? If we don't hurry now, the sun will set on our way home. And it gets pitch black at night in the mountains, you know," Momoko said curtly.

I didn't have a response for that.

"We'll take a little break a little farther ahead. Keep it up a bit longer," Momoko said to encourage me. Then she walked on briskly.

It was after midday when we finally took a brief rest beside a clear mountain stream. We divided up the onigiri the innkeeper had packed for us, so we each had two. Listening to the soothing sound of water in the dappled light that streamed through the trees eased my weariness a little. I took several deep breaths of that pure mountain air, trying to catch my breath. Momoko still seemed perfectly well composed. She had a placid expression on her face as she bit into her onigiri.

"Momoko, you're really in good shape."

"Takako, as young as you are, you really have no endurance."

I laughed, and teased her a little. "Momoko, you'll probably be in great shape even when you're that old lady's age."

Momoko laughed. "Honestly, it doesn't look like it's going to turn out that way. I'm sick. And pretty soon I'll start to fall apart."

"What?" I said.

"Okay, break's over. Just a little farther to go," she said, sounding all fired up as she walked away.

Sick? How could Momoko be sick? She doesn't look sick at all . . .

Momoko turned back and saw me still standing there. "If you don't get a move on," she called, "I'll leave you behind!" She looked so small at this distance from behind. I rushed to chase after her.

After that, we devoted our attention to hiking and hardly exchanged a word.

At one point, we went down a rugged slope that was just bare rock, then circled halfway around the mountain, and went up another slope. We went up and down, again and again, on our route. My poor feet were screaming in pain.

Then, all of sudden, the sky opened up before us, and the summit came into view. On the peak, the viewing platform looked sort of like a flan resting on a plate. There were a few pines scattered around an expanse of reddish-brown earth. Ahead of us was the steep drop-off of the cliff. The only other visitor was a middle-aged man, sitting on a bench mounted right next to the edge of the cliff. Everything around was quiet and calm. We sat down together on the bench across from the man. The gentle breeze, coming straight at us, began to cool our burning muscles.

The view from the mountaintop was definitely impressive. We were surrounded by green as far as the eye could see. Everywhere you looked there were mountain peaks pressing up against each other. And the sky felt unbelievably close. So endless and clear. If I stared at it too long, I felt like it might swallow me whole.

When I squinted, I could just make out the city of Tokyo. It was so small it looked like a little speck in the distance. I tried to imagine that tomorrow I'd be back living my life again in that little speck, but here on the mountain I couldn't believe that life was real. Wouldn't it be better to just stay here and live like this? It felt like it. I wondered if Momoko had the same thoughts the first time she came here.

"Hey, Momoko?"

"Yeah?"

"What made you decide to leave Satoru?"

I wasn't asking because my uncle wanted me to. I just wanted to ask her. And this time I hoped Momoko would actually answer me. All of a sudden it felt like she would.

"Hmmm . . ." she nodded slightly, staring straight ahead. As I waited for her to say something, I stared straight ahead like her, not saying a word. A swallow flew across the sky above us without making a sound.

"I told you about the person I was in love with a long time ago, right?" she said, still facing forward.

"Yeah."

"Well, when I was with him, I got pregnant. I'd always wanted a family so badly, so when I found out I was unbelievably happy. He didn't share my joy at all though. Well, that's because he already had a wife and kid back in Japan. I found that out afterward."

A strong gust of wind blew in and swirled up a cloud of sand. A moment later, everything fell silent again.

"If I'd been stronger, I might have been able to save the baby at least. But I wasn't. I didn't have the confidence to find happiness by causing someone else so much pain, or the courage to pay that price and go on living. Afterward, I regretted it so much I wanted to die. But, by that point, it was too late." She sighed a little and smiled faintly.

"Then I met Satoru and we got married. Satoru was desperate to have kids too. But somehow we were never blessed with them. Ten years passed and then we were given a child at last. Satoru was happy too. I was so happy I cried. But before the baby was born, it died inside me. I felt like I was being punished. And I was being punished because back then I had let my baby die. I felt like I didn't deserve to give birth now. Satoru tried his best to comfort me. I'm sure it was hard for him too. He's so ridiculously kind. You already know that though, right, Takako?"

I nodded.

"After that, I managed to get back on my feet somehow, and

the two of us worked hard together to revive the Morisaki Bookshop. Satoru was careful not to say another word about the baby. And then he became more and more absorbed by running the bookshop. I liked the shop, and I liked to think that I could love Satoru the way he loved me. But that wasn't enough. No matter how much time passed, the sadness never went away. I was carrying this feeling around—like there was a gaping hole left open inside me. And instead of disappearing, the emptiness inside me seemed to grow day by day. I started to think that being with him when I was feeling this way was almost a betrayal. Then I woke up one day and realized how far I'd let things go." Momoko let out a long sigh. It was like she'd been holding her breath until she finished telling me the story. "If he wants to look down on me for doing something so selfish, what can I say? I can't argue with him. That's why I've been afraid to talk to him about it. I mean you seem pretty shocked."

How could I possibly respond? I had no idea what to say. There's probably no way at this point in my life for me to imagine the pain she felt. I could understand only the intensity of feeling. In the face of something like that, any easy words I might offer seemed meaningless. I could only sit there beside her, shaking my head in silence.

After a while, Momoko got slowly to her feet. "Sorry to bore you with all this. Let's hurry back."

That's when I noticed the light was starting to fade on the mountain ridge across from us.

On the way home from the summit, Momoko moved so quickly that she ended up ahead of me again. I had so much on my mind that I was lost in my own thoughts the whole way. Thanks to which, I lost my footing a few times and fell hard on my butt.

By the time we got back to the inn, I was exhausted. It was already fairly dark outside, and at some point it had even started to drizzle. There was still an hour before dinnertime, so we went straight to the bath.

I soaked for a long time in the hot water, staring up at the ceiling in a daze. It had been a really long day. When I looked out the window, the view was already giving way to a deep darkness. The milky white steam rising from the bath drifted outside like it was being swallowed up by the night.

The clatter of a door being flung open caught me by surprise. When I looked over, I saw Momoko standing there in the steamy haze, totally naked. Now that she'd stripped off her clothes, she looked even smaller than usual.

"Can I come in?"

"Um . . . sure . . . please," I started to say, but she came in without waiting for my reply.

"You're so young, Takako. Your skin's so nice and fresh," she said, having a look at me in the bath.

I automatically turned my back to her. "I'm not that young," I said.

"Oh, you've still got a lot ahead of you. I mean look at that gorgeous curve from your neck to your chest. As you get older, your age tends to show there. But your skin is still so nice and smooth. I'm jealous," she said, eyeing me with a little smirk.

"This totally counts as sexual harassment," I said.

"Oh, don't worry, Takako," she said, laughing loudly. The sound of her laughter reverberated pleasantly inside the walls of the bathhouse.

When she first walked in, I'd noticed the fairly painful-looking scar from her operation running vertically about ten centimeters down her stomach. Although she hadn't made any attempt to hide it, I still felt like I'd seen something I shouldn't have. I looked away. It made me think of what she'd said earlier in the day about what had happened to her and about the emptiness she felt inside. It felt hard to talk, like I had something stuck in my throat.

After she was done washing, Momoko got into the water beside me and closed her eyes contentedly. "Ah," she said, "that feels so good."

As I looked at her face in profile, I felt a strange impulse to take her in my arms and hug her. "What's that?" I said, pointing out the window. The moment she was distracted, I leapt. But Momoko must have sensed me coming because she nimbly eluded me.

"What? What're you doing?" she shrieked.

"Nothing," I laughed, splashing as I came closer, slowly but steadily backing her into one end of the bath, like a border collie running down a wayward sheep.

"What is it, Takako? You've got a crazy look in your eye."

Ignoring the sound of fear in her voice, I pounced. Then I closed my eyes and held on tight. Her shoulders felt very small and very warm.

"Wait a . . . what are you . . ." She fought me off frantically. Water was splashing everywhere. Waves spread over the surface of the bath. But I didn't loosen my grip.

Finally, she seemed to understand and gave in. Her body relaxed, and she let her head rest on my shoulder.

"I give up. I didn't know that's what you wanted, Takako," she said as she leaned on me.

"You weren't paying attention."

We both let out a laugh, but we stayed like that for a long time, at one end of the big bath, holding each other.

9

Our second night was much quieter than the first. The guests we'd met the night before had already gone back down the mountain. In their place were a man and a woman who seemed to have just arrived that day. The couple talked quietly to each other through dinner. I found myself hating them. Why did they have to come to a boarding house like this place? They ought to be at one of those hot spring inns where they could do what they wanted and keep their relationship a secret.

The innkeeper came in carrying a serving tray and discreetly turned on the fairly ancient television in the middle of the room. I think there was something wrong with the volume, because the sound of people laughing on screen would suddenly cut out, disappearing inside the cathode-ray tube of the TV. When that happened, the room seemed even more silent than before. I found the way the sound cut out weirdly scary, and eventually I got up, went over to the TV, and turned it off.

We went back to our room and lay under the covers of our futons, side by side. Once we turned off the lights, it felt terribly quiet. The rain seemed to have stopped too. We could no longer hear the sound of rain falling in the distance.

"Let's not rush to leave in the morning," Momoko said quietly.

"That sounds good," I said, but my mind was elsewhere. I was staring up at the ceiling in the dark. Momoko had told me before that she couldn't sleep if there was even a small light on, so it was pitch black in the room. And yet as I lay there with my eyes open, gradually getting used to the dark, I could make out the silhouettes of things in the room, however dimly.

A moment later, I called out softly to Momoko, whom I knew had to be right next to me though I couldn't see her. "Are you awake?"

"Yeah?" She answered right away as if she was awake too.

"Can we talk for a second?" I asked in a quiet voice, still staring at the ceiling.

"Sure. I kind of feel like talking too."

"It's about what you said this afternoon . . ."

"What were we talking about?"

"Being sick . . ."

"Oh yeah." She had paused for a moment before she answered.

"Is it—is it really bad?" I asked the question in one breath like I was reading a line from a script. My voice sounded so helpless in the dark.

"Yeah. If you think of it like that, it's pretty bad. But if you think about it another way, it's not so bad."

"What do you mean?"

"Hmmm . . ." Momoko drew out the sound until it became a groan. "What I mean is, you know how there are people who die unexpectedly in an accident or from a sudden illness, and they never get the chance to say goodbye to anyone? Well, maybe, compared to them, I'm really fortunate. I still have time for all that."

"You mean . . ."

"Nah, it's nothing to get so worried about. It's not like I'm about to die right now or anything. A little while ago, I went into the hospital and they removed my uterus and did a bunch of other things, and now I'm going regularly to the hospital, and they're figuring out my prognosis. I think it's just something I have to keep an eye on for the next few years."

"And is that why you went back to my uncle?"

"It's not like I decided to come back as soon as I found out I was sick. The thought didn't even occur to me at first. But then I had this dream one day when I was in the hospital and feeling pretty depressed."

"A dream?"

I rolled over to face Momoko in the dark. But it was too dark to see the expression on her face.

"In the dream I was on a boat that was right about to leave the harbor. No, actually, I think I might've been the boat. Anyway, I was paddling out toward the horizon. I could see all the way out there in the distance. I knew for certain that once I got there, I was never coming back. When I turned around, I saw a man standing in the harbor, waving at me. I could tell at a glance that it was Satoru. I had this feeling deep down that we would never see each other again, so I tried with all my might to wave back at him. But my boat was too fast—Satoru grew smaller and smaller as I left him behind. Before I knew it, I'd lost sight of him, and I was alone, drifting across the ocean. That was the dream." I could hear Momoko rustling her covers as she turned to face me. Then she laughed for a moment.

"It's embarrassing, but when I woke up from that dream in my room at the hospital, I started crying, and I cried so much I couldn't believe it. I mean I knew it was just a dream. But the tears kept coming, one after another. In the end, I was sobbing. I can't even remember the last time I cried before this. That's how rarely I cry, but that day I was just a total mess. I was so, so sad. It was unbearable. And then I knew I wanted to see Satoru again, no matter what. It's weird, don't you think?"

"I don't think so." When I tried to imagine how lonely she must have felt then, I kept shaking my head. I couldn't see her going through something like that.

"It's definitely weird," Momoko declared. "But that's why I came back, even though I still felt ashamed."

"So that's what happened . . . but you're still not planning on talking to my uncle about your illness?"

"Nope. Not planning on it," she replied flatly.

"Why not?"

"At this point, I don't want to be a burden to him now."

"He's much stronger than you give him credit for."

"You're right. Of course he can handle it. That's not the issue. It's about his feelings. I can't do that to him. It wouldn't be fair after everything that's happened."

"But if you don't try to tell him—" Momoko interrupted me before I could say, "you'll never know."

"I made my decision the moment I decided to come see him."

"But . . . but . . . then you told me." I realized my voice was getting louder.

"I guess I wanted to tell someone after all," Momoko said softly. "I just wanted to open up to someone . . . about leaving . . . about getting sick. And I knew that if I asked you not to tell Satoru, that you would keep my secret."

"That's not . . ." I said, my voice breaking as I started to cry. "That's not fair."

"You're right. It's not fair. I'm sorry, Takako. It made me so happy when you hugged me in the bath. I was truly happy. You're a really kind girl. That's why Satoru and I love you so much."

I buried myself in the covers as tears ran down my cheeks. I kept repeating the words over and over again. *It's not fair . . . It's not fair.* Momoko kept saying she was sorry. But I went on repeating the phrase dozens of times. And I kept on going until, at some point, I cried myself out and fell asleep.

The next morning under an overcast sky, the innkeeper and Haru saw us off. Just as she had when we arrived, Momoko stood in the entryway and bowed formally to the innkeeper. The innkeeper laughed as she tried to get her to stop, but Momoko persisted. "See ya!" Haru said casually and waved goodbye.

Momoko was back to her usual cheerful self in the morning. On our descent, she talked cheerfully. "Oh look, the lilies are blooming . . . The leaves are starting to show some color over there." When I replied, I tried my best to be as cheerful as I could. I didn't know what else to do.

We parted ways at Shinjuku Station that evening. With the crowds teeming around her, Momoko stood in front of the turnstile and bowed deeply to me. "Thank you, Takako," she said. "I had a really good time." The smile on her face was almost dazzling. Looking back at her, I took a risk and asked, "What are you going to do now?"

"I'm going back to the bookshop."

"No, that's not what I mean. I mean after that."

Momoko said, "Hmmm . . ." and folded her arms. "I'll figure something out." That was all she said. Then she turned briskly on her heels and disappeared into the crowd.

I stood there staring, even after I lost sight of her small figure in the crowd. I tried to imagine what might happen next, but the feelings it stirred up in me were more than I could bear.

10

Uncle Satoru called two days later, sometime before noon. When I saw his number show up on my cell phone, I could already imagine what had happened.

"Sorry to bother you at work," he said in a low monotone as soon as I picked up. "There's a letter waiting for you when you come by the shop . . ."

So that's what happened. I let out a long sigh. I shouldn't have let her go off like that. Yet even if I had known that this was going to happen, what on earth could I have done?

Momoko didn't play fair. I knew that. As I squeezed my cell phone in my hand, I could feel the anger welling up inside me.

"Takako?" I hadn't said anything for so long that my uncle called out to me, starting to doubt I was still there.

"I'm coming right over."

"What about work?" my uncle was asking when I hung up.

It's not fair. It's not fair. I kept repeating the words over and over again in my head as the train carried me to Jimbocho. *It's not fair. This isn't how adults act.* I could understand some of what she was feeling. To be missing in action for five whole years, and then suddenly return only to say you're sick. I could see how you might hesitate to say something. But if she really still loved my uncle, then that was all the more reason to tell him. And what was going to happen to my uncle once she'd left him again? It had been hard enough for him the last time she left without saying anything.

I was on my uncle's side. Just as he had been on my side all this time. And that's why I couldn't forgive Momoko for disappearing again. The anger kept welling up inside me. I couldn't contain it. I was so angry. I was angrier than I'd ever been before. My body was trembling.

When I got to the bookshop, my uncle showed me the note she'd left for me.

It said, "Thank you. Please take care of yourself."

I tore it into little pieces and let them fall on the floor.

My uncle stared at me, dumbfounded.

"It's not fair. It's cowardly. I can't believe her. She only showed me her good side, and then she left. She just ran away."

"Takako?" My uncle was peering at me with a look of concern. "Um, Taka—"

I interrupted my uncle right there, and, with my head held high, announced to the room, "I'm breaking my promise. Actually, it wasn't even a promise. She just told me not to say anything."

"Huh?"

My uncle sat there with his mouth hanging open as I told him the short version of what Momoko said to me that night. I was well aware, of course, that all this would come as a shock, but he had a right to know. And there was no one else who could stop Momoko.

And yet my uncle didn't appear shocked. When I finished telling him, he just gave a little nod and said, "Okay."

"You knew?"

"Not at all."

"But then . . ."

My uncle sighed deeply and tried to sit down and almost fell into his chair. "I knew it would've taken something pretty significant for her to come back. Like I said before, once she makes a decision, she doesn't change her mind. So for her to show up again despite that, well . . . That's why I was afraid to ask too many questions. Which is why I asked you. How stupid am I? I never just talked to her directly, and this is the result," he said. He sounded like he had already given up.

I got up close to him, looked him straight in the eye, and said, "There's still time. But if you let her go now, you truly will never see her again. Even if you don't know how everything will turn out, you can't let her go. Do you understand what I mean? The only person who can stop her is you."

"Okay . . ." That was all he said. His voice lacked any conviction.

"So hurry up and get going!" I said, raising my voice. "Uncle, you remember when you told me not to run away from everything? It's just as bad if you and Momoko do it too. I'll watch the store. You go to her."

"But I don't know where to find her . . ." He still had a look in his eye like he felt powerless to stop her.

"Nothing comes to mind? Some place Momoko would think to go first?" I asked.

He stared at me for a moment, looking dumbfounded.

"Nope."

"It can't be. There's got to be someplace. Momoko's your wife."

"That's true, but I'm telling you . . ."

"Try thinking of a place that's special to her."

My uncle stared at me blankly for a long while, then suddenly he said, "Oh! There is one place. Maybe—no, it's got to be there."

"You've got it?" I asked again.

"I do. I might just make it there in time," he said, nodding forcefully now.

He almost flew out of his chair. "Takako, can I ask you for another favor?"

"Sure."

"I'm not paying you for the hours, right?"

"I know that, you idiot!" I shouted. There was no time for this stupid routine. My uncle finally went running out of the store like I'd given him a kick in the pants.

I hoped that he would be able to stop her this time.

I stood in the doorway of the store and watched as my uncle bolted down Sakura Street. He seemed to get smaller and smaller as he ran. Unfortunately, because of his bad back, the scene was interrupted a few times by him stopping to thump his lower back, but that's how it goes, I guess.

After my uncle disappeared from view, I stood for a while in a daze looking up at the narrow band of sky visible through the gap between the buildings on the block. It was that same aqua-blue autumn sky—with little, dappled clouds drifting slowly across it like a school of fish.

"What happened? The store's open, right?" A middle-aged man had stopped in front of the shop. He gave me a curious glance and then ducked inside.

I followed him in. "Welcome to the Morisaki Bookshop," I said. I'd played my part. Now the rest was up to my uncle.

I sat down at my old spot at the counter and waited for Momoko and my uncle to return.

11

The trees on the street had already dropped the last of their leaves when I saw Wada again.

That night, I stopped by the Saveur for the first time in close to a month. I hadn't felt much like going for a while. Even when I'd passed it on the street, I just walked right by. But as the weather turned colder day by day, I found myself craving their coffee.

I opened the door and said, "Oh."

Wada was sitting at a table in the back. Our eyes met right away. He had noticed me too. I thought, I screwed this up, didn't I, and tried to get away with just a quick hello, but he stood up conscientiously and waited for me to come over.

"Nice to see you," I said, feeling a bit flustered as I sat across from him.

"It's been a while," he replied with his usual cool tone.

The waitress brought over water and asked, "Are you ready to order?"

At the moment, I was still thinking I could just say hi, then change seats and order my coffee. So I said, "Not yet." She nodded and walked away still smiling.

It was a little while before Wada spoke. "How have you been?"

"Um, okay, I guess? And you?" I replied.

"So-so," he said cheerfully and took a sip of his coffee.

Was he still waiting for his ex-girlfriend to show up? But he'd told me himself he was done with that. Just as that thought crossed my mind, Wada suddenly said, "I've been waiting for you." Then he reached into his bag and took out a paperback. I realized it was the Saneatsu Mushanokōji book I'd left behind that night before my trip, *Friendship*. So much had happened, I had completely forgotten about the book.

I would've never dreamt that Wada had it.

"You held on to it all this time for me?" I asked as he handed me the book.

"That night I noticed the book after you'd left. I asked the owner if he would give it to you the next time you came in, but he said he didn't know who you were. He claimed he'd never seen you before."

There was no way the owner didn't know me. We'd seen each other dozens of times. I was basically one of the regulars.

"That's how I ended up holding on to the book. I didn't have a way to contact you, so I've been stopping by from time to time to see if you were here. My timing must've been bad though because I never ran into you. I felt guilty about it, but just waiting got boring so I ended up reading your whole book."

I listened to him tell me all this with my mouth hanging open. And then I saw the owner standing at the counter, and I finally understood what had happened. He was polishing the glasses, pretending not to recognize me. I watched him closely until our eyes met for an instant. *Well, that was dumb. He probably had no idea that Wada was waiting for someone else. He'd gotten all worked up over nothing.*

"I'm so sorry for all this," I said, and bowed to Wada.

"No, honestly it was a nice opportunity for me to read a book that wasn't *Up the Hill*. I should be the one thanking you," he said with a playful laugh.

After this strange twist, I felt like I couldn't hold back any longer. I looked down and felt my shoulders start to tremble.

"Are you okay?" Wada watched me with a worried look on his face. But when he realized that I was just laughing, he started laughing too. Little by little, we were starting to feel comfortable with each other. I realized that in my heart I was genuinely delighted to see him again. It's true. Seeing him made me incredibly happy. It didn't matter what he felt about me. It was pointless to worry about that. There was nothing I could do to change that fact.

"Um," I said, looking up at him again, "I'm glad to see you."

I couldn't leave without thanking the owner. I felt that deeply. Without his help, I really might never have seen Wada again. Even if I ordered a hundred cups of coffee, I would still be in his debt.

"I'm glad to see you too," he said. "I mean if I hadn't, I would've been guilty of larceny, so there's that. No, that's a lie. I wanted to talk to you again." He laughed, scratching the back of his head in embarrassment. I was so embarrassed I couldn't look at him. Instead, I glanced out the window and saw a reflection of the two of us, face to face. Outside, the fierce winter wind was blowing, and it looked awfully cold. I was deeply grateful that the two of us had been able to run into each other again.

"Well, now," Wada said, stretching happily. "Let me pick up the tab today to thank you for lending me the book. That wouldn't bother you, would it?"

I held up a finger and smiled. "Well, okay, maybe just one cup."

"Still being modest?" He pretended to act shocked for a moment, then he turned to our waitress who was walking by and waved her over.

12

The Morisaki Bookshop stands alone at the corner of a street crowded with used bookstores. It's tiny and old and really nothing much to look at. There aren't many customers. And because it has a limited selection, people who aren't interested in its specialty never give it a second glance.

But there are people who love this store. And as long as they're devoted to it, then that's enough. That's what my uncle Satoru, the shop's owner, always says with a smile. And I agree. Because I love the bookshop and its owner.

Today, I'm off from work and on my way to visit Jimbocho for the first time in ages. My uncle called me last week. From the excitement in his voice on the phone, I knew something had happened even without him telling me.

"She said she wanted to see you too. It's been so long," he said. Her condition had been improving, and at the moment, things seemed good. It was a relief to hear that, at least for the time being. And the thought of seeing the two of them after so long made me walk a little more quickly up the busy street.

That day my uncle went running after her, Momoko didn't come back to the bookshop. But my uncle was able to find her. He went to the temple where they'd held the memorial service for their stillborn child. He said that when he found her, it looked like Momoko had been standing by the spring in the back of the temple for a long time. I didn't dare ask for the details of what they said to each other. That's between the two of them. But they couldn't have told each other any lies in that place where their child lay sleeping. For them, what was probably most important was that they each came clean about their feelings. It's possible that somewhere in her heart she wished my uncle had come and found her in that same place when she'd left him five years earlier. "When she saw me coming, she collapsed on the spot. She cried out like a little child and started bawling. In that moment, I loved her from the bottom of my heart. Tears were streaming down my face. I felt like I was finally able to face all the things I hadn't noticed before, all the things I'd turned away from. I took Momoko in my arms, and I said 'Don't go' over and over again. 'I need you.' Before I saw her there I couldn't have said something as simple as that."

When he returned to the shop alone late that night, he talked me through what had happened. Rather than being depressed that she wasn't with him, he seemed quite cheerful. "She promised," he said at the end. "The two of us will talk things over, and then one day she'll come back. She made me a promise."

Then, a whole year later, Momoko returned. She said she'd needed to get her thoughts in order first, otherwise it wouldn't have been fair to him. He told me that's what she'd said when they said goodbye that day. She was as strong-willed as ever.

After crossing the busy road, I go down Sakura Street. On this narrower backstreet, I pass a row of used bookstores, and then I can see my uncle's shop right ahead of me. The door clatters when I fling it open and find Sabu holding court at the counter. "Hey, Takako," he says and waves me over.

"Oh, Sabu, you're here? Where's my uncle?"

"That's not the warm reception I was hoping for from you," he giggled. "He just left on a delivery."

I hear a cheerful voice coming from behind him. Looking around, I see a small woman with short hair sitting behind the counter.

"What happened to your hair?" I say.

Momoko raises her hand and touches the close-cropped hair above her ear. "Oh, I cut it. Honestly, when I first thought about it, I really wanted to get a buzz cut, but Satoru stopped me." She laughs loudly.

"It looks good on you," I say and sit down next to her. It truly does look good on her.

"You think so?" she frowns.

The store around lunchtime is pretty slow as usual. Aside from the fact that Momoko is there, nothing much has changed. And that makes me a tiny bit happy.

"By the way, Takako, what's this about you having a boy-friend?" Momoko asks in her usual abrupt way.

"What? Who'd you hear that from?"

She points a finger at Sabu. "Just now, from him."

"No, I heard it from the owner of the Saveur," he says, and starts giggling again as if something were funny.

"Are you cooking him some of the dishes I taught you?" Momoko asks with a grin.

"No—I mean, yes, but not . . ." I stammer.

That doesn't satisfy Momoko. She keeps interrogating me un-til I cry, "Come on, isn't that enough?"

At that moment, I hear the sound of the door opening. My uncle is back.

"Oh, Takako, you're early," he says.

The moment he walks in, Momoko says, "Hey, Satoru, did you know Takako has a boyfriend?"

"What? I hadn't heard anything. Is that true? Why didn't you tell me?" He comes over and looks me in the eye. "You know you can discuss it with me, right?"

"That's right," Momoko says, clapping her hands together. "And if Takako marries him, then he can take over the shop. After all, we need to find a successor."

For some reason, the thought of this makes my uncle completely lose it. "That's nothing to joke about," he yells. "Why should I let that guy take over?"

"If you haven't even met him yet, how do you know who he is?" Momoko says coldly.

Sabu giggles. "Well, maybe it's time for me to go home," he says. "See you soon, Momoko." He waves to her and leaves the store in quite a cheery mood. He doesn't say goodbye to my uncle or me.

Once Sabu is gone, I say, "It didn't take long for you to have him wrapped around your finger, did it?" I'm amazed.

"Hey, I didn't mean to. I just talked to him," Momoko says nonchalantly.

"They've been at it all this time. I mean, of course, she won him over. Sabu didn't stand a chance." My uncle says this so matter-of-factly that Momoko and I burst out laughing.

Then Momoko suddenly gets to her feet and turns toward me.

"Momoko Morisaki has returned home and is reporting for duty." She gives a brisk military salute.

I quickly stand up straight.

"Welcome home," I say. "We've been waiting for you. And if you disappear again, I really will be angry with you."

"You're the one who broke your promise. Honestly though, I'm grateful for what you did. Thank you, Takako. Let's be friends again," she says and then she laughs as she pinches my cheek. I'm so used to it at this point that just like my uncle, I cry, "Quit it!" but I'm already starting to give in.

"Maybe I should cook something special tonight for Takako to show my gratitude." Momoko thumps her chest proudly. "Will you come shopping with me?"

"Of course, your cooking is the real reason I came," I say with a smile.

"Takako, before you go," my uncle cuts in, "I was thinking about what we were talking about earlier . . ."

We ignore him and walk out the front door.

Outside, the sky is clear. A few large clouds drift pleasantly overhead. I stretch my arms up high and shut my eyes for a moment. I can feel the warm sunlight pressing on my eyelids.

"Hey, if you don't hurry up, I'm leaving you behind."

I open my eyes when I hear her voice.

Up the street, Momoko turns back to look at me. The sun glints off her new short hair and she smiles.

"Come on, come on," she says, waving to me. And then she dashes ahead.

For a moment, I watch her from behind as she walks away. Then I run down the street after her.

Translator's Note

When Satoshi Yagisawa's novel debuted in Japan, it won the Chiyoda Prize, named after the district that is home to Tokyo's beloved Jimbocho neighborhood of bookshops. In the course of the story, he catalogs the many pleasures of reading: the joy of discovering a new author; the hedonism of staying up too late to finish a book; the surreptitious thrill of getting to know someone by reading their favorite novel; and the freedom of walking into a bookstore and scanning the titles, waiting for something to catch your eye.

Any reader who goes looking for all the books mentioned in these pages might not find everything, but that's to be expected, especially in little secondhand places like the Morisaki Bookshop. As far as I know, *Until the Death of the Girl*, the book by Saisei Murō that sparks Takako's passion for reading in chapter 4, has not been translated into English—*yet*. But the book that played the same role for her friend Tomo, Osamu Dazai's *Schoolgirl*, is available in a recent translation by Allison Markin Powell. It shouldn't be difficult to track down English editions of Jun'ichirō Tanizaki's, Ryūnosuke Akutagawa's, and Sōseki Natsume's well-known books, particularly *Kokoro*, one of the most loved novels in Japanese literature. You can find stories by many of the other authors Takako discovers in the major anthologies of Japanese short stories, each of which is almost a bookshop unto itself.

This translation owes its existence to many people, especially its eminent editor, Sara Nelson, and Setsuko and Simon

Translator's Note

Winchester, without whom I never would have met Sara. I could not have done it without my parents: my father, Yuichi, who answered every question I had, and my mother, Susanne, who first taught me the pleasure of reading. The text was immeasurably improved by my whole family, particularly my brother-in-law, Bruno Navasky, and my sister, Melissa, who each read multiple drafts, and by my friends Hiroko Tabuchi, Junko Suzuki, and Ayaka Kamei, who patiently offered their insights. I would also like to thank my wife, Nicole, whom I met one day by chance in a bookstore and who is always my first reader.

If you loved *Days at the Morisaki Bookshop* then you might enjoy *The Door-to-Door Bookstore*

Carl may be 72 years old, but he's young at heart. Every night he goes door-to-door delivering books by hand to his loyal customers. But when his job is threatened he and nine-year-old Schascha – who insists on accompanying him – work to restore Carl's way of life, and return the joy of reading to his little European town.

The Door-to-Door Bookstore is a heartwarming tale of the value of friendship, the magic of reading, and the power of books to unite us all

A Man for All Seasons

It has been said that books find their own readers—but sometimes they need someone to show them the way. Living proof of this could be found at a bookshop in southern Germany, that went by the name of the City Gate. Admittedly, the name was an unusual choice, since the actual city gate—or at least what remained of it, which even locals often mistook for an avant-garde artwork—stood a good three streets away.

It was a very old bookshop, constructed and extended time and again over numerous historical periods. Extravagant architectural ornament and stucco rubbed shoulders with unadorned right angles. The glorious juxtaposition of the old and the new, the flamboyant and the restrained, which characterized the building's exterior also continued into its interior. Red plastic stands of CDs and DVDs stood next to frosted metal shelves of mangas; these in turn took their place next to globes displayed in polished glass cases, or elegant wooden shelves of books. Customers could find board games, stationery, tea, and even chocolate—a recent addition—for sale. The labyrinthine room was dominated by a heavy, dark counter known to employees simply as the Altar. It looked like a relic from the Baroque period: carvings on the front depicted a rural scene of a hunting party astride magnificent steeds, a pack of wiry dogs alongside, in pursuit of a group of wild boar.

Inside, one late summer's day, the question that is the raison d'être of every bookshop was being asked: "Can you recommend a good book?" The questioner, Ursel Schäfer, knew exactly what constituted a good book. Firstly, it must be gripping enough to keep her awake in bed reading until her eyes drooped shut. Secondly, it must contain at least three, preferably four, points at which she was moved to tears. Thirdly, it must have no less than three hundred pages, but no more than three hundred and eighty, and fourthly, the cover must never be green. Books with green covers were not to be trusted—bitter experience had taught her this on several occasions.

"Certainly," replied Sabine Gruber, who had been manager at the City Gate for the past three years. "What kinds of books do you enjoy reading?"

Ursel Schäfer did not wish to say. She wanted Sabine Gruber to know; after all, as a bookseller, she was surely naturally endowed with a certain level of clairvoyant skill.

"Give me three keywords, and I'll find just the right one to suit you. Romance? Rural? Cozy? Yes?"

"I wonder—is Mr. Kollhoff here?" asked Ursel Schäfer, her tone uneasy. "He always knows what I like. He knows what everyone likes."

"No, I'm afraid he's not here today. Mr. Kollhoff only works for us occasionally now."

"What a shame."

"Never mind, I have something for you. A family saga, set in Cornwall. Look, the cover art shows the family's stately manor and grounds."

"It's green." Ursel Schäfer stared at Sabine Gruber in reproach. "Bright green!"

"That's because the story is set on the Earl of Durnborough's grand estate. It's had very good reviews!"

The heavy front door opened stiffly, setting the little copper bell above it tinkling brightly. Carl Kollhoff folded his umbrella, gave it his habitual shake, and placed it in the stand. His gaze scanned the bookshop he called home, on the lookout for new literary arrivals awaiting an introduction to his customers. He'd always likened himself to a beachcomber, who needed only a single glance to spy a hoard of treasures ready to be seized and freed from the grainy sand. As his gaze lit upon Ursel Schäfer, however, the treasures were forgotten in an instant. She threw him a warm smile, as though he were an amalgam of all the charming men she'd fallen in love with in the pages of the books he'd recommended over the years. In reality, Carl resembled none of those characters. He'd once had a small paunch, but over the years it had receded, much like the hair on his head, as though they'd entered into a pact to disappear together. Now, at age seventy-two, he was lean, but continued to wear his old, now-oversize clothes. His former boss, Sabine's father, had told him he'd begun to look as though his only source of nourishment was the words in hisbooks, which were notoriously low in carbohydrates. "But rich in substance," Carl had always responded.

Carl wore rugged, heavy shoes of thick black leather with soles solid enough to last a lifetime. Good socks were also essential, in his opinion. These he combined with olive green overalls, and a matching collared jacket.

On his head, he wore a narrow-brimmed fisherman's hat, to protect his eyes from rain and bright sunshine. He never took it off, even indoors, other than to sleep. Somehow, he felt less than fully clothed without it. Nor was he ever seen without his glasses, the frames bought from an antique shop decades ago. Behind them peered shrewd eyes which bore signs of a lifetime of reading too long in poor light.

"Ms. Schäfer, how lovely to see you," he said, stepping toward

Ursel Schäfer just as she took a step toward him, and away from Sabine Gruber. "May I recommend a book that would make ideal bedtime reading?"

"I so enjoyed the last one, especially when they gazed into each other's eyes at the end. A kiss would have been even better, to seal the deal, but on this occasion I'll settle for a gaze."

"It was almost more intense than a kiss, don't you think? Some gazes can be."

"Not when I'm doing the kissing!" For a moment, Ursel Schäfer felt deliciously wicked—a rare occurrence for her nowadays.

"This book," said Carl, taking one from the pile next to the till, "has been waiting for you since the moment it was unpacked. Set in Provence, and every word scented with lavender."

"Oh, Bordeaux-red books are the best! Does it end with a kiss?"

"Have I ever given an ending away?"

"No!" She pouted, but took the book from his hand.

Carl would never dream of recommending a novel without a happy end to her, but on no account would he rob Ursel Schäfer of the tiny thrill of wondering whether this one would be different.

"I'm so glad there are books in the world," she said. "I hope that's one thing that never changes! So many things do, and it happens so fast. Everyone pays with plastic money now. People give me such odd looks whenever I count out the right change at the till!"

"The written word will always remain, Ms. Schäfer; sometimes there is simply no better form of expression. Print is the best preserving agent for thoughts and stories; it keeps them fresh for centuries."

With a warm smile of farewell, Carl Kollhoff stepped through a door covered with advertising posters into a room that served as both stockroom and office for the bookshop. Inside was a desk barely visible under stacks of books and an old computer monitor framed with yellow Post-its. An enormous calendar covered in red pen dominated the wall.

As always, his book orders were waiting in a black plastic crate in the darkest corner of the room. In former times, their place had been on the desk, but since Sabine had taken the bookshop over from her father, the crate had migrated a little farther each day toward the least accessible corner. In tandem with its migration, the crate's contents had gradually reduced. Few people needed book delivery these days, and every year, their number continued to dwindle.

"Hiya, Mr. Kollhoff! What did you make of the game? That was never a penalty! The ref must've been blind!"

Leon, the new work experience lad, exited the tiny staff toilet, followed by a cloud of cigarette smoke. Anyone else would have known it was utterly useless asking Carl such a question. He never watched the news, never listened to the radio, never read a newspaper. He would have been the first to admit that he had lost touch with the world. It had been a deliberate decision, once all the reports of incompetent state leaders, ice cap melt, and suffering refugees had begun to sadden him more than the most tragic literary family saga ever could. It had been a form of self-preservation, even though his world had shrunk as a result. The world he now inhabited measured no more than two-by-two kilometers, and he patrolled its borders every day.

"Have you read J. L. Carr's fantastic book about football?" asked Carl, preferring to ask a question than to take sides on an issue of referee competence.

"Is it about our club?"

"No, it's about the Steeple Sinderby Wanderers."

"Never heard of them. Don't read books anyway. Only if I have to. In school. Even then, I try to watch the film instead." Leon grinned, as if this was a cunning way to make a fool of his teacher, rather than himself.

"Then why are you doing work experience here?"

"My sister did the same. Three years ago. We live around the corner—it's a short walk to get here."

Leon was to work at the bookshop for two weeks, as was customary for most students in Germany. He neglected to mention that anyone who failed to find a work experience place was forced to spend the allotted two weeks helping the caretaker, who would use the time, and a selection of suitably humiliating tasks, to take his revenge on the whole school body—as represented by the work experience students—for all the graffitied walls, old chewing gum stuck under desks, and discarded half-eaten packed lunches.

"Does your sister enjoy reading?"

"After she came here, sure. But that won't happen to me!"

Carl smiled. He knew exactly why Leon's sister had taken to reading. His former boss, Gustav Gruber, now a resident at the Münsterblick care home, had known exactly what to do with reluctant readers like Leon and his sister. He would set them to dusting each individual plastic-wrapped greeting card, one by one. The student in question was guaranteed—out of sheer despair at the tedium—to reach for the nearest book, which of course had been strategically deposited within easy reach by Gruber himself. Gustav Gruber had converted them all. He had always been good with children. To Carl, children had always been unfathomable creatures, even back when he himself had been one. And the further he left his own childhood behind, the more strange and peculiar they seemed to him.

Old Gruber had tempted Leon's sister with a novel in which a young woman falls in love with a vampire. For Leon, clearly brimming with raging hormones, Gruber would have left out a book with a beautiful teenage girl on the cover, and large-print pages. "It's important that they read, not what they read," old Gruber had always said. Carl couldn't quite endorse that view for all books: the ideas found between the covers of some were worse than poison, but more often than not, there was healing to be found on the page, sometimes even for ailments the reader hadn't realized they were suffering from.

With great care, Carl pulled the crate out from its corner. There were only three books lying forlornly inside. He took out brown paper and string to pack each book individually, as though it were a gift. Sabine Gruber had told him on numerous occasions he shouldn't bother, and to spare the expense, but Carl insisted. His customers would expect it. In a reflex action Carl was entirely unaware of, his hand stroked each cover before wrapping the books in the thick paper.

Finally, he picked up his olive green army backpack: marked with all the wear and tear of Bundeswehr use, but still in good condition thanks to Carl's care. Although it was empty, the fall of its cloth clearly indicated emptiness was not its natural form. He gently lowered the books between the heavy folds of the backpack, which he had lined with a soft blanket, as though he was carrying tiny puppies to their new owners. He arranged the three books in the backpack with the smallest resting farthest away, while the largest nestled next to his back, where it would not be compromised by the curve of the backpack.

As he was leaving, he paused, then turned to Leon. "Please

would you dust the greeting cards? Ms. Gruber would like that. Best to bring them in here, then you can work in peace. I've always done it at the desk." Whisking Nick Hornby's Fever Pitch from the shelf where he'd spied it earlier, he laid it on the desk. The football pitch was a luscious shade of green—Ursel Schäfer wouldn't have given it a second glance.

* * *

Carl called it his round, although it resembled more of a polygon around the city center, without right angles or symmetry. The path traced by the ruins of the old city wall, standing like stumps of teeth in an old man's gums, was the boundary of his world. For thirty-four years, he had not set foot outside it; everything he needed in life lay within its borders.

Carl Kollhoff spent a lot of time walking, and he spent as much time thinking as he did walking. Only when he was walking could he think clearly; perhaps his footsteps on the cobbled streets were the one thing that could set his thoughts in motion.

A person walking at ground level might not notice it, but every pigeon and every sparrow knew the city was circular. Every old house and alleyway was oriented toward the minster, the cathedral which rose majestically in the center. If the city had been part of a model railway, you would say the minster had been built to the wrong scale. It dated from the short period in which the city had become very rich, a period that had come swiftly to an end before the minster could be completed, leaving one of the towers truncated still.

The houses stood reverentially around the minster; some of the older roofs even leaned at a deferential angle. They kept a respectful distance from the main entrance, allowing space for the largest and most beautiful square in the city: Münsterplatz.

As Carl stepped into the square, the feeling crept over him, as it had on previous occasions, that he was being watched, like a deer in a clearing, standing helplessly in the hunter's sights. He had to smile—in no other respect could he have been accused of resemblance to a deer. The aroma of the city was at its most intense in Münsterplatz. In the seventeenth century, the city had been besieged, and according to local legend, a baker had created the sugared wheel: a doughnut in the shape of a spoked wheel, filled with chocolate cream and sprinkled with powdered sugar. He took it to the besieging army, an edible message that they should leave. In reality, the calorie-dense confection had not been invented for a further two hundred years, a fact backed by documentary evidence, but the old story continued to thrive, and the city's visitors were eager to believe it.

Every day, Carl trod the exact same cobblestones of Münsterplatz in slow, even paces. If there was ever a person in the way, he would wait, increasing his stride afterward to regain the lost time. He had mapped out his route across the square so carefully that it could even be followed on market days. He had also ensured it traced a course that maximized his distance from the square's four bakeries, since he could no longer stomach the smell of the hot, greasy sugared wheels.

He turned into Beethovenstrasse, which in honesty was no more than an alley, not at all worthy of the great composer. An entire district had been named after famous composers, courtesy of an employee at the planning office who had wanted to make his own mark. The widest street had been reserved for Schubert, the employee's personal favorite.

Although Carl Kollhoff was not aware of it, he stood at that moment at the exact center of his world. It was bordered on two sides by tram lines, the 18 and the 57. (In fact, the city only had seven tram routes, but it had been felt that higher numbers would add a nice metropolitan air, at least to its public transportation.) On another side was the fast road from the north, and on the fourth was the river, which for most of the year was content to burble picturesquely, and only surged to high water for a few days in the spring, rising to emit a modest roar, like a lion cub with underdeveloped vocal cords.

His first call of the day took him into a lane by the name of Salierigasse, to the home of Christian von Hohenesch. A pedestrian hurrying by would not have noticed the dark stone villa's grandeur: it stood a step back from the other buildings, crouching like a hunched black swan waiting for its moment to spread magnificent wings. Behind it lay gardens bordered by a square of gigantic oak trees, with three benches positioned to enable Christian von Hohenesch to read with the sun falling on his book at any time of day.

Carl was aware that Hohenesch possessed enormous wealth, but not that he was the richest man in the city. No one knew, least of all Hohenesch himself, who never compared himself with others. His family had made their fortune generations ago in the tanning trade by the river, and succeeded in not losing it again during the industrial revolution. Christian von Hohenesch had no need to work; he allowed his shares and investments to work for him. He simply managed his wealth managers. A housekeeper came once a day to cook and clean the few occupied rooms; a gardener came once a week to trim the hedges and maintain the sun's passage to his books; a caretaker service visited once a month; and from Monday to Friday, Carl came with a new book, which Christian von Hohenesch had usually finished reading by the following day. As far as Carl knew, Hohenesch had not stepped beyond the borders of his kingdom in an eternity.

Carl pulled on the copper rod by the door, and a bell rang a low note in the villa's interior. As usual, there was a pause while the householder walked the long, dark corridor; then the heavy door creaked open, just a crack. Christian von Hohenesch never stepped outside. He was a handsome man: tall, dark-haired, with sculpted cheekbones, a striking chin, and a sadness that settled over his features like fine gray dust. As always, he wore a dark blue double-breasted suit with a fresh white orchid in the buttonhole, and his black leather shoes shone as if he was dressed for the Opera Ball. Hohenesch was much younger than his clothing suggested: barely thirty-seven years old—but he had worn suits since early childhood, and they felt as natural to him as jeans did to others.

"Mr. Kollhoff, you're late. We had agreed a quarter past seven," said Hohenesch by way of greeting.

Carl bowed his head in acknowledgment, then carefully reached for his backpack. "I've brought your new book." He straightened the string's bow, which had shifted on the journey.

"I hope it lives up to your recommendation." Hohenesch took the book, but did not unwrap it. It was a novel about Alexander the Great, set during his time under Aristotle's instruction. Hohenesch read only philosophical works.

He handed Carl a tip, calculated according to the book's weight, which he had researched in advance. "Please be punctual again next time. Punctuality is the politeness of kings."

"Of course. Enjoy your evening."

"Yes, I hope yours is equally pleasant, naturally."

Christian von Hohenesch closed the solid wooden door, and the villa once more appeared deserted.

The master of the house would have loved to discuss books and authors in depth with Carl, whom he regarded as an educated, well-mannered man, and a kindred spirit. But with the passage of time, the words of invitation had escaped him. Perhaps he had lost them among the many rooms in his grand home.

Carl took his leave of Christian von Hohenesch—yet in his mind, it was another person altogether he left behind. Everywhere in the real world, Carl saw reflections of novels. To him, the city was populated with characters from books, even if those characters lived in quite different times, or far-off lands. To Carl, the moment Christian von Hohenesch had first opened the heavy door of his villa, he had stepped out from the pages of *Pride and Prejudice*. Carl was now bidding farewell to Pemberley in eighteenth-century Derbyshire, and to its owner, Fitzwilliam Darcy, who, despite his impeccable manners, could at times appear harsh and arrogant.

Carl's inability to remember any name, unless it belonged to a book character, had begun during his school days, when so many of his classmates had given their teachers nicknames, most of them unflattering: Loobrush, Prince Morphine, or Spitty. Carl had given them different names: Odysseus, Tristan, or Gulliver. Unlike his classmates, when he graduated high school with his Abitur qualification and the offer of an apprenticeship at the bookshop, his habit of assigning nicknames had persisted. The young lad slouching along in a threadbare uniform every day as Carl made his way to the bookshop became the Good Soldier Schwejk. The greengrocer who sold him apples transformed into the wicked queen from *Snow White*—mercifully, she refrained from poisoning her fruit. At some point, Carl had realized that his city was full of literary figures; every inhabitant had their literary counterpart. In the years that followed, he met Sherlock Holmes, head of the murder squad in the city police; he even met Lady Chatterley, who often opened her door wearing a flimsy robe, and for whom he developed a slight crush as a young man. Sadly, she left the city with Adso of Melk. Captain Ahab obsessed over an enormous mole which wreaked havoc in his garden, and which he consistently failed to hunt down. Carl delivered books about South America to Walter Faber, a chronically ill engineer, right up until his death. And in an apartment building that had once been a prison, the Count of Monte Cristo lived behind barred windows, a feature which the new owners had on a whim decided to retain.

He found that a suitable literary name always occurred to him long before he succeeded in memorizing the real one. It was as though his memory wished to prevent him from burdening it with anything so profane. From the moment he selected a name, he ceased to see the real one. On their way from his retina to his brain, the letters of Christian von Hohenesch would be miraculously transposed into Mr. Darcy, entirely without Carl's awareness. Only in very particular situations would his mind relent and provide a real name—and these days there were precious few it needed to recall.

Carl's route through the winding alleyways next took him to a literary figure with a fate far bleaker than that of the Pemberley gentleman whose story concluded with a happy marriage.

His client was waiting behind the door, peering through the spyhole at the few passersby in the street beyond. No one came here for a stroll. No one came to admire the buildings; the handsome architecture stopped several streets away. In this part of the old city, pedestrians increased their pace, as though they could not bear the oppressive narrowness of the street, with its gables looming overhead, threatening to close ranks and block out the daylight.

The slender young woman behind the spyhole knew at what

time Carl would arrive. She also knew that it was foolish to spend long minutes peering through the door, instead of waiting in the living room for the doorbell, but she was unable to tear herself away. Andrea Cremmen brushed a lock of blond hair behind her ear and tugged her dress straight. From the time she started kindergarten she had always been the prettiest girl in the room, a quality which had earned her both affection and envy—and an early marriage to Matthias, a man with a promising career in the insurance industry, who worked long hours in the evening and on weekends to give them a comfortable life. Andrea herself was a trained nurse, but now worked half days at a small doctor's surgery, where she had been put behind the reception desk, because the sight of her calmed and lightened the spirits of the patients. No one had needed to tell Andrea to smile; she did so quite naturally—it was part and parcel of being pretty. A pretty person who doesn't smile looks arrogant, so she smiled all day.

She had never dared to look anything other than perfect. What would happen then? What would others see in her? But Carl Kollhoff seemed like a man to whom she could show her unsmiling face. He would find the right words to describe what appeared there. Andrea knew that he chose his words as carefully as a perfumier selecting ingredients for an expensive scent. She let her smile drop, and pulled the lock of hair forward, permitting herself a few strands of disarray.

Spotting Carl in the street, she tucked the strands swiftly back behind her ear again.

Carl rang the bell, and waited. He knew Andrea Cremmen always took a little time to open the door, and was always slightly breathless—but she always wore a smile of pleasure.

A key rattled in the lock, then the door opened.

"Mr. Kollhoff, you're early today! I hadn't expected you yet.

I must look in a terrible state." She ran her fingers through her glossy hair, styled to perfectly complement her elegant dress in a red rose print.

Carl found her bewitching, and yet the sight of her always made him feel a little sad too. Behind all her beauty lay something he could not quite put a finger on—but it had something to do with the package he now handed to her: one of the books Andrea Cremmen loved so well. The book's weight was perfectly acceptable (Carl liked books to have the appropriate weight: heavier than a bar of chocolate, lighter than a liter of milk); it was the weight of the contents that gave Carl concern.

"Is it a good one?" she asked, pulling the string on the packing paper straight.

"From what I've heard, The Shadow Rose lives up to the author's other works."

"Highly dramatic?"

Now it was Carl's turn to smile. There was an unspoken agreement between them: when he brought her a book, it was always dramatic, with a tragic end. In the past, he had occasionally recommended books with a happy end, but she had never enjoyed them. She found they bore no relation to reality. Andrea Cremmen loved novels in which the female protagonist suffered and either died or was left unhappy and alone at the end. Open endings were only acceptable if they held out the possibility of one or the other.

"As always, I retain my right to silence," said Carl. "How did you like the last novel?"

Andrea Cremmen took a deep breath and shook her head. "It was so sad! She walks into the water at the end… Why didn't you warn me?" She gave a playful pout.

"I can't possibly do that."

In the past he had packed her books in bright, cheerful gift wrap, but after a while that had felt disingenuous.

"Will you bring me another next week? I've heard about a novel where it's night all the time—it takes place in Greenland in the winter. And the main character has lost her child. Do you know it? I thought it sounded good."

Carl had heard of the book. He'd hoped Andrea Cremmen hadn't.

"I'll bring it." Carl didn't say he'd bring it gladly, because that would have been untrue.

"Can you interest me in anything else?"

"There's a crime story set right here in this city; it's only just been published. I've not read it yet, but I hear it's very funny."

Andrea Cremmen waved the suggestion aside. "Do you think I'd enjoy it?"

Carl made a point of never lying. Send a lie out into the world, and you can never retrieve it. "No."

"I don't think so either."

"But it might make you laugh. And you have a beautiful laugh—I hope that's not too forward of me. I'm sure you've-heard what Charlie Chaplin said, 'A day without laughter is a day wasted.' We have so few days on this earth, we can't afford to lose any." He'd never said anything like this to her before. Perhaps he'd sensed her unhappiness was greater than usual today? Carl didn't know. Sometimes his mouth just went ahead and said things without consulting his head.

Andrea Cremmen was no longer smiling. Her lower lip trembled slightly. "You've saved my day, thank you!" The door closed abruptly.

Carl watched the door close, not on Andrea Cremmen but on Effi Briest: a sorrowful young woman, married too young, whose sad fate was every bit as tragic as that of the numerous heroines in the books Andrea Cremmen ordered. Carl wished he could do more for her than deliver books that proved others can suffer too, but without any guidance on how to end the suffering.

Behind the door, Andrea Cremmen suppressed her tears. She longed to tell him what had happened that day, but that would have entailed reliving it, which was more than she could face. She unwrapped the package with trembling hands and had begun reading the book before she left the hallway. One of the characters had taken their own life by the end of page one.